What Does a Christian Look Like?

Essays on the Reality of God and His Love for Us

Suzanne E. Ybarra

Acknowledgements

My thanks go to my entire family, including my son Dillon, Antoinette, Alison, Flavio Lombardo, Sonia, Pablo, Manual, Delia, Delia, Paul, Irma, Joe, Norma, Tony, Sylvia, Raul, Nancy, Destina, Adolfo, Cathy, Peter, Isabella Yolanda, Robert, Florence, Nancy, Michelle, Nancy, Leo, all the Ybarras, Victory Outreach pastors, sisters, and brothers.

Thank you for your encouragement to be who God has called me to be.

Table of Contents

Preface: Note from the Author

Dear Reader,

In the forty-nine years that I have been a Christian, I have experienced God's faithfulness.

Before I knew Jesus, I was going to church and youth group meetings. My mom sent me so I would have a social life. God used the opportunity to give me spiritual life. My high school youth group friends prayed me into the kingdom of God.

The day I met Jesus was a normal day for my family. My parents were arguing. They had not divorced yet. I was hiding, sitting on the floor beside my bed. I told God, "If you're real, I need you. Please come into my heart."

I am on an adventure with God. One time He kept me from being attacked. Foolishly, I was walking alone on a dark night in a deserted park. Two men came toward me and walked past me. I heard one say to the other, "See, we should have." The other said, "No."

There was a time when I was despairing because of work. I feared I was going to hear, "You're fired." God kept assuring me of His presence. One day He met me at a flower bush. The day before this encounter, I had finished my lunch and didn't want to go back to my desk. While I waited for the dreaded moment that I would have to go back to work, I doodled squiggles, connecting lines, and darkened areas inside elongated shapes. It was nothing intelligible until the next day when I was walking home from work. In someone's front yard, a bush caught my eye. I examined it closer and was astounded to see the flower petals were what I had doodled, and the bush as a whole looked like the other doodles I had done. I felt God's voice breeze through my spirit, telling me He was with me.

The love God demonstrates toward us is the love talked about in the Bible. Isaiah 65:1 (NIV) says, before I asked for God, He revealed Himself to me. Psalms 103:11 (NIV) says God's love for us is higher than the heavens are above the earth.

Most of these stories were columns I wrote for *The Woodburn Independent*, a local newspaper. Beginning in 2007, it was a monthly column. In 2011, the editor restructured the newspaper and invited me to submit future columns as an occasional guest columnist. Recently and repeatedly, God told me to put my columns into a book. I am finally obeying. He gave me the title. I knew it was Him speaking. This book is full of true stories of Christian faith and behavior.

I have grouped these stories according to their main point. In this way, you can find the ones that address your need or interest. I have included publication dates for columns initially printed in the newspaper.

For all your days, I encourage you to go for God. An adventure awaits!

Sincerely,
Suzanne E. Ybarra
November 2021

Who Are You?

I have been crucified with Christ [that is, in Him I have shared His crucifixion]; it is no longer I who live, but Christ lives in me. The *life* I now live in the body I live by faith [by adhering to, relying on, and completely trusting] in the Son of God, who loved me and gave Himself up for me.

Galatians 2:20 (AMP)

Baby Steps to Big Ideas

What's the big idea? Have you ever been asked that? The person asking you was probably not asking with the same care and interest that I am extending to you. I want to know, "What's the big picture? What do you dream about? What do you want to do with your life?"

I can picture you. You are either tall or short, a man or a woman, young or old, a person of color or not. Actually, it doesn't matter what you look like. What matters is what your heart looks like. Do we know what our hearts look like? I spend most of my time in my head, thinking. That's why I appreciate the following exercise. I'll walk you through it. First, think about something. For example, think about what you're going to eat for your next meal. Then, feel an emotion. The emotion does not need to be associated with your thoughts. It could be any emotion: love, sadness, or happiness. Now, switch back and forth between the thought and the emotion. Notice where your focus is when you're thinking. Where is your focus when you're feeling? With thoughts, you're in your head, and with your emotions, you're in your heart. Right? Is that your experience?

Here's my point: if you spend more of your day in your head, like me, rather than in your heart, then you might need this exercise to help you go to your heart whenever you want to. The heart is an enjoyable place to rest. Also, it's easier to dream when you are in your heart.

I invite you to visit your heart and look ahead. What good things do you want for your loved ones? What good do you want to give others? What positive impact will you have on this world? How can you make that impact more widespread, more encompassing of everyone?

While you are in your heart, is there a dream tucked away in a corner? This is just me writing and you reading. Do you feel safe enough to go to that corner of your heart and look at your dream? You can pick it up and hold it close. You can cradle it in your arms.

13

You can sit quietly with it. When you're ready, you can gently put it back in its protected place.

Dear Friend,

If you have a desire to do something more or different than what you're doing, take a baby step. Baby steps are tiny, but each one is a triumph. I have a baby living at my house right now, and she's learning to walk. She loves to put her hands in mine and walk around the house. She's wobbly, and her steps are uneven, but she trusts me to help her. Your steps may be small, wobbly, and uneven, but they'll be accompanied by the joy of accomplishment as you start the momentum toward your goal.

One last point: who's going to hold you up and keep you steady while you take your baby steps? Why not ask the one who said He would never leave you? He's all-powerful. He knows your future. He loves you more than you can imagine. His name is Jesus.

July 2008

Will You Marry Me?

They say more people get married in the summer than any other season. I don't know if they are right. My husband and I met in December and wed the following March. Our timing is probably not typical, but we've been married for more than twelve years. Time has demonstrated the validity of our decision.

In a little bit, I want to tell you about a marriage proposal I got from someone else. In the meantime, let me tell you about one of the final scenes in the movie *Raiders of the Lost Ark*. The bad guys lift the lid off the ark of the covenant. An essence arises from the ark. It looks wispy and harmless, but it becomes a forceful zap. It takes just a moment for each bad guy to be zapped and become a puddle. These guys had searched for the ark because they were greedy for power. I guess they did not think it through about the ark being God's house. If you go to God's house, you're likely to encounter God. I like this movie scene. It's accurate according to the Bible, and it shows us what we have.

Psalm 97:4–5 (NIV) talks about God and His enemies. It says, "Fire goes before him and consumes his foes on every side. The mountains melt like wax before the Lord." Also, regarding the ark, there was that time when one of the king's men touched the ark. He was not authorized to touch the holy things. He died on the spot (2 Samuel 6:7).

I realize this aspect of God can be frightening. Here comes the good news: God's goodness, mercy, and love are available to us. We saw this aspect of God when Jesus came preaching, teaching, and healing. He showed compassion. He cared so much, He wept. He loved people. In John 8, there's a story of the religious leaders who dragged an adulterous woman to Jesus. They wanted permission to stone her. Instead of condemning her, Jesus gently points out to the religious that they too are sinners. He told the woman to stop sinning. He let her go.

When we have Jesus, we don't get the God of justice. We don't get death. We have life because Jesus took the zapping headed our way: on the cross. It's that important to have Jesus. It's also an adventure to be with Jesus. Picture this, if you will: I am at a conference center for a week with a small group of Christians. I have been a Christian for more than ten years, and I enjoy going on spiritual retreats. I am immersed in learning more about God and spending time with Him in prayer.

One afternoon I am in my room, alone, on the bottom bed of a bunk bed. I am looking over my life. I ask God, "What do you want me to do with my life?" I hear inside myself a question, "Will you marry me?" At first, I am surprised, shocked even. I know Who is asking, but the question is unexpected. I make a little joke, "What are your prospects?" Then I regain my senses and say, "Yes."

It has taken me years to grow into the idea of being Jesus' bride. According to the Bible, the church is Jesus' bride. For me, I see life as a process of becoming a bride. It's a long process, and I'm not totally there yet.

How about you? Do you know the church is Jesus' bride? Can you see yourself as His bride? His proposal is on the table. Go for it.

August 2008

Even if Only for You, He Would Have Endured the Cross

I didn't tell anyone for a while because I thought I was the most special person on the planet. I didn't want to hurt anyone's feelings by telling them they were not the center of the universe: I was. Ah, pride. It slides right in and makes itself at home. I have a defense for my pride, though. I understood Jesus telling me that even if I had been the only person on earth, He still would have endured the cross. Have you seen Mel Gibson's movie, *The Passion*? Even if you haven't, you can imagine the pain that goes along with being beaten and then crucified. Jesus was tortured. He would have gone through it even if it had been just me who needed him to do it.

Do you understand why I feel so special? Jesus loves me tremendously. Now I can talk about it because Jesus feels the same about you. On a Christian program, I heard a man say Jesus would have died for him, even if he had been the only one to die for. I thought, *Woah! Jesus is telling other people too!* Then, last night I read an autobiography by Jean Lovelace Zeiler. She was a Broadway actress in the 1950s. She was introduced to Jesus through a co-worker. Then, she wanted her husband to know Jesus. She didn't push or prod him but lived the example of a changed life. When he decided he wanted to check Jesus out, he listened to a pastor who told him that he just had to believe that even if he were the only man on earth, Jesus still would have come and died for his sins. This was in the 1950s. Apparently, Jesus has been telling people this for decades.

I guess it shouldn't surprise me that we are all super-sized special to Jesus. He's not limited to loving just one person, one neighborhood, or one country. He's not like men. He's God. Now that I've looked at all this, a little light came on. I wish it had stayed off. With Jesus saying He would have died even if I'd been the only one to die for, He is also saying my sins were enough to nail him to that cross. I cannot point an accusing finger at the Hitlers and terrorists, blaming them for the crisis of the cross. It was me. I don't feel so proud anymore.

WHAT DOES A CHRISTIAN LOOK LIKE?

I can only apologize for my failings. *I'm sorry, Lord.* And be grateful for His love. *Thank you, Jesus.*

Even this week, I have seen God's love in action. My husband got some quality help with a project he's working on. With that help, his project will be complete in a third of the time it would have otherwise. Also, some friends and I prayed for a little girl who was at death's door. She is recovering and going home now. My sister-in-law had spots on her lungs. We were concerned because she's been a smoker for years. Many people prayed for her. When she returned to the doctor, he didn't find any spots. Her lungs are clean now. Praise God.

God is in the little and big things: from helping with our projects and health to not suffering in hell. And I'm not the only most-special-one on the planet. You are too.

August 2009

God Is Real

Once upon a time, there was an eight-year-old girl who had her own bedroom filled with stuffed animals, books, and other things little girls enjoy. She had a dog who would sleep at the end of her bed every night. She knew that even though nighttime monsters were probably hiding in her two closets, her dog would keep her safe. So, under her queen-size feather cover, Valentine slept soundly.

One afternoon, when she was about ten, Valentine was in her bedroom when she heard music playing downstairs in the living room. Over and over, the same spot on the record was being played. It was, "Why, why, why, Delilah? Why, why, why, Delilah?"

Valentine went down to see what was going on, and her dad only said, "Oh, I didn't know anyone was home."

Looking back, Valentine pieced together her family's story. When her dad was obsessing over a song about betrayal that day, it was likely the same day his wife told him about her affair. In all fairness to his wife, Valentine's mom, I must tell you that she didn't really cheat on him. She was feeling neglected in her marriage, so she told her husband she was having an affair. I suppose she wanted to arouse his jealousy. That's what Valentine figured out later after she grew older and talked to her mom about her life. When she was ten, however, Valentine was innocent of the ways of a man and woman.

In the innocence of growing up, Valentine only knew she was loved. Her mom took her and her two brothers to the movies, SeaWorld, and Universal Studios. Her mom helped each of them with their homework. She sent them off to school with little notes in their lunches. She made all of Valentine's school clothes. Her dad took her on walks and worked hard for his family every day.

By age sixteen, Valentine was not as innocent. She still knew she was loved but knew that something had to change, or she was going to go crazy. At dinner, her dad would tease her mom about being

At this conference, I was seated between my husband and a 275-pound, heavily tattooed Mexican dude. To me, he looked big and dangerous. I wondered what I was doing there. I was new to Victory Outreach, and this was my first world conference. Was it going to be my last? And then, my Mexican brother opened his mouth to join in singing worship songs to God. His joy was evident. He sang his love for his savior. I realized he was a big teddy bear. I calmed down.

Today, I attend Victory Outreach in Salem. My pastor, Joseph Islas, has a history of rebellion before meeting Jesus. His nickname was Al Capone, and he was a heroin addict. But he had, as he says, a praying mama. Twenty-eight years ago, Joseph was finally sick and tired of being sick and tired. He cried out to God, "I need a way out. Show me the way out." God showed him.

July 2010

Risk for the Eternally-Significant

Did you lose $20? I found it. I was looking through my journal the other day and found the money. I had forgotten I put it there, but it makes sense that it was there: I put nuggets in my journal. I have gold nuggets of wisdom, encouragements, quotes, facts, and questions to consider. Life happens fast. I use my journal to record points I want to review or ponder.

What would you do if you found an extra $20? Buy lunch? Or maybe you'd stash it in your sock drawer. Or maybe $20 is not enough to get excited about because it doesn't come close to this month's electric bill. If $20 isn't the answer, let's look at what else is in my journal.

I made notes about the book *Heaven is Real: Lessons on Earthly Joy - From the Man Who Spent 90 Minutes in Heaven*. The author, Pastor Don Piper, was in a fatal car accident. During his hour and a half of being dead, he went to heaven. After he was prayed for and came back to life, he went through months of surgery and painful physical therapy. He still lives with pain, and it is his perspective on pain I'd like to share with you. See what you think.

Piper urges us to keep going. Don't give up. If we believe God keeps our lives intact until we accomplish our God-given purpose, then we can hold on. God is a miracle worker. Even if we hold on for five minutes at a time, that five minutes might be what the fight is all about. Don't surrender. Do you believe God has a plan and purpose for your life? He says He does. Do you believe Him? Do you believe He can keep you going until you accomplish His purpose for your life? Is God powerful and creative enough to do that? What is His plan for your life? Do you think His plan could be to love you now, love you forever and ask you to tell your friends He loves them too? That sounds like the God I know.

One time, God gave me an image of a big sickle harvesting wheat. It was like He was telling me the time of judgment is coming. His myself questions: Would I like the ring? Would it fit? Was this a God thing? I slowly ripped into the package and found a little black box. Inside was a sparkling, beautiful ring. The opal is a good size, and the ring fits just right. And putting it on, I heard in my spirit, "With this ring, I thee wed."

When I was in my twenties, I asked Jesus what He wanted me to do with my life. He asked me if I would marry him. My first response was, "What are your prospects?" I followed that quickly with, "Yes." I thought the wedding was going to happen that week or at least that month. I didn't know there was going to be a decades-long engagement period. Someday Jesus will take His bride, the church, home. Until then, I have a tangible reminder of Jesus' intimate love. Isn't it a miracle the God of the universe wants us as His bride?

Written May 2018, unpublished

I Am One Who Lives in the Presence of God

Who are you? Throughout my day, others decide who I am. To my husband, I am intelligent, funny, and cute. When I walk into a store that sells baby clothes and toys, the clerk sees my purse and graying hair. She pegs me as a potential customer, looking for something for my grandchild. Downtown on my lunch hour, those I walk by see a white female, walking casually, available to make eye contact. I am not a threat. Back at my desk after lunch, I'm a responsible worker.

For practical reasons, who I am is determined by where I am and what I'm doing. We need each other to behave according to the context we are in. If I were to go to work and ask a coworker where the train sets are, they would look at me funny, unless I asked my co-receptionist, Patty. There's an overlap. If you asked Patty about me, her telling would be similar to what others see. And because I asked her where she bought one, she could even tell you I'm looking for a train set. But I wish none of this mattered. Practicality aside, what if our culture was different? In church, we sing, "Jesus is the center of it all." Ephesians tells us we are God's children, free, with Holy Spirit living inside us. Together, believers are the temple of God.

In King Hezekiah's time, he repaired the temple of God. He brought in the priests and encouraged them to stand before and serve God (2 Chronicles 29:4). As believers who pray for others' needs, we behave as priests. As we help others, we are serving God. Every time we obey Holy Spirit's leading, we are saying yes to God and His lordship. Do you agree?

Knowing we are the place where God lives, how can we sit still? We are not here just to survive and thrive. We are to proclaim! When someone asks who I am, I want to be able to say, "I am one who lives in the presence of God." King David said it about himself. Why can't we say it too?

In Psalm 27, David declared he was in God's presence. There is nowhere we can go that God is not there. God is everywhere. Psalm

41 says God set David in His presence forever. That same relationship is available to us. Psalm 89 says we will walk in the light of God's presence as we praise Him.

I know this can sound foolish. Do you want it anyway? In God, we live and move and be. I want to shout out the reality and goodness of God. This column is a proclamation. I believe God will honor my desire for additional opportunities to stand and serve. God willing, I will keep you updated on what happens next.

November 2017

Family Is Everywhere

I didn't grow up in a large family, but now I have so many family members I can't even count them. It's wonderful. I don't know all their names, but I enjoy our connections. Recently, one brief connection gave me a long-lasting smile. I was standing on a street corner holding signs. One sign had an arrow and said, "Car Wash." The other sign said the name of my church. As a man drove by with his car window down, he turned up his car radio to blast out a Christian song. At another fund-raising car wash for my church, a man made his donation and then brought us a case of water to share with our customers. It was during a heat spell. That man provided refreshment for brothers and sisters he probably won't even meet until heaven.

Sometimes I recognize a sister before we are introduced. It startled me the first time it happened. I was going into an office she was leaving. In the doorway, instantly, my insides signaled recognition. I am more familiar with the phenomenon now. My spirit recognizes kindred spirits.

Last week, my husband, Gilbert, and I participated in a mini-family reunion at Rainbow West Bookstore in Salem. It started when I called the store to find out where they were. They are no longer on Lancaster Drive. A very helpful woman answered the phone and explained they had moved across the street, almost right next to a Target. We found the store and the young woman, Ruth, who had answered the phone. I was reassured. Several Christian bookstores have closed down, but not this one!

Ruth, my husband, and I had a nice visit, a blessing of a chat. While Gilbert and I were shopping, an older woman came in and had a short and sweet visit with Ruth. I didn't eavesdrop, but I do have good hearing. They shared some details about their lives. After they hugged, they introduced themselves to each other by name.

That's how it is with family. The connection of love does not need to know names. It doesn't need persons to be of the same generation to relate. It doesn't need cultural similarities to feel at ease. Of course, I'm not asking for every trip to the bookstore to include long chats. During the short time we were there, Ruth also helped a man looking for a large print Bible. She asked a few questions to determine which Bibles he would appreciate and then offered him several to choose from.

What I am asking is, if I gathered up one hundred strangers, how many of them would I be related to? When we don't know each other, we see the outside and how different we are from each other. What would it be like if we could just as easily see the inside of others? How much similarity would we find? Can we get past appearances to discover realities?

September 2018

When Were We First Known by God?

When were we first known by God? My cousin was asked that question in a class she's taking at her church. Let's look at that. The debate on abortion asks, "When does life begin?" Some answer that life begins when the baby can live outside, separate from the mother.

In contrast to this is a conversation I had with Marie Chinn. I called Chin because I was curious about Life Chain, and she is associated with Salem Right to Life. Chinn said the little one in the womb has a heartbeat at three weeks. At six weeks, brain activity. Another source, Dr. Maureen Condie, PhD, speaking before Congress, said eight weeks is "the earliest point at which the fetus experiences pain in any capacity."[2]

Thus, we have a practical answer and answers from science. Where is God in all this?

Christian abortionist Dr. Willie Parker says, "I became morally convinced that it was not a conflict of my Christian values to provide abortion care, and in fact, it became unethical to me not to do so."[3] Parker believes he is doing God's work and that he is protecting women's right to decide their futures for themselves and to live their lives as they see fit. In contrast, Chinn shared about Life Chain, an annual event where people line up along Lancaster Drive for an hour. They hold signs that say, "Abortion kills children," "Jesus forgives and heals," "Abortion hurts women," and "Pregnant? Need Help? Call 800-712-HELP."

Chinn has experienced God's presence. One year, on the day of Life Chain, it was pouring unending buckets of rain until the event started. It stayed dry for the hour-long vigil. After Life Chain time was over, the rain resumed full force. God has answered Life Chain's efforts. One year, a young woman carrying a baby shared her story with a woman on the line. She had been pregnant. Her entire family was pressuring her to get an abortion. She saw the sign that said, "Abortion kills children." She decided she didn't want to kill her baby.

The question is, "When were we first known by God?" The abortion debate points toward an answer. Scripture is not silent. It satisfies our quest. In the first chapter of Jeremiah, God says He knew us before He formed us in our mother's womb. In Psalm 139, God saw us before our bodies were formed.

Along with Psalm 139, there is an amazing detail in Ephesians 1:4. It says God chose us before the creation of the world. The answer is God knew us before the creation of the world. The next question is, "How does this answer affect the way you see yourself and others?"

March 2019

Who Are You? Why Are You Here?

As a child, I read. Reading took me on adventures. Reading was someone talking to me personally, a friend. In the newspaper, I'd read the comics and the advice columnists. I still read the advice columnists. I have never felt like writing them until now. Last week, I read a letter from a woman who sounded at wit's end, and the columnist's response missed the mark. I was writing my own response before I put down the newspaper.

The woman writing in said she liked the idea of hanging on to one's personal purpose when life is overwhelming, but she had nothing to hang on to. She was not enthused about her job; she was not a parent, spouse, or best friend to anyone; she did not have any meaningful hobby or volunteer job. She asked, "Why am I even here?" She signed off by disclosing she is in therapy and on medication and her last question, "How?"

The columnist encouraged her to think back to what tiny treasures her life has held and revisit those as often as she can. For example, where does she like to shop? What is her favorite meal? What was she doing the last time she forgot what time it was? These are helpful questions, I admit, but do they match the level of angst the writer was confessing?

I don't know if she'll print what I emailed her, but I sent the following to the columnist:

Dear Columnist,

I would like to respond to the letter about finding purpose in life. Therapy and medication have their place in helping people, but psychology can't tell me the purpose of my life. It is theology that answers the questions: Who am I? Why am I here? How do I get through the hard times?

Theologian and author Bill Johnson says we start by finding out who we are and what our purpose is. After that, we can mature into

WHAT DOES A CHRISTIAN LOOK LIKE?

having a fulfilling life. He wrote a book rich with practical wisdom *When Heaven Invades Earth*.

Rick Warren, the author of *The Purpose Driven Life*, offers hope for the question, "What on earth am I here for?" We are not accidents. There is a reason for everything. There is a place we belong. His book is easy to read and includes discussion questions to stimulate thought.

I offer these suggestions with the hope that those looking for answers will find the beauty and treasures of life. Thank you for your time and consideration.

If the person who wrote for advice sees this, then I say, "Hallelujah!" If you need encouragement, I hope you got some here today.

May 2019

What Determines Who You Are?

Who are you? What determines who you are? Is it the way you look or the work you do? Is it your family? Your choices and thoughts? Race, culture, or gender? If you said "Yes" to any of these options, let me ask you another question. Would you still be you if all your hair fell out? If you changed jobs? What if you got married, divorced, reunited, or adopted children? What if you decide to go to a bar? Or church?

Would you still be you if you thought you are unworthy of God's love? What if you thought you are His favorite?

What if your skin color changed? Do you go through your day thinking, *I'm this color, so I have to go there, do that, and be this?* Society tells us what we can and cannot do based on our skin color and gender, but are we a color or gender in our depths?

I've never told myself, "I'm a girl so I can only like the color pink, and I have to think about how to make the prettiest bouquet of flowers." I'm being silly here just to make my point: I don't research what women are supposed to do and then force myself to do those things. I do not consult my gender to direct my behavior.

I'm asking you about your essence. Who are you deep down? For example, J. Andrew Kirk wrote about what church is. The church's essence is mission: reaching out to others with the good news of Jesus Christ. The church is outreach. Sharing the good news is so deep inside the church that it defines who she is. What is so deep inside you that it defines who you are?

Do an exercise with me, please. Direct your attention to your mind. Notice your thoughts. Then direct your attention to your heart. Notice your feelings. Gently repeat. Notice your thoughts. Go to your heart. Notice your feelings. Next, consider who is noticing your thoughts and feelings. Mentally take a step back and look at what you just did. Who was noticing your thoughts and feelings?

I asked my son to do the above exercise. At first, he said he was the sum of his experiences. I then asked him who was having the experiences. We had a good conversation. For our conversation, here and now, I offer a couple more clarifying questions. What, if taken away from you, would change who you are? Or asked another way, if everything about you and your life changed, what one thing would have to remain the same for you to still be you?

July 2019

You Are Special to God

I don't know how it started, but I love geese. Their honking is music to me. Their flying in formation is a wonder. Their long necks and big wings are grace in motion. Which came first, my love for geese or God using geese to get my attention and love on me? I don't know.

I know there have been times when I've been troubled, and then I hear the honking. I hurry outside or stop in my walking and look up. There they are, reminding me God loves me. He sends me geese to tell me so. When I see geese, I receive them as a greeting from God, an encouragement, or just a reminder of God's existence.

I know I sound a little unusual, but you can relate, right? When you see a rapturous sunset, don't you tell God, "Good job! That's beautiful, God!" After driving around the parking lot for five minutes and then remembering to ask God for one, don't you thank God? Or when the accident in the intersection happens ten minutes before you get there, you see God's hand of protection, don't you?

On top of all these ways of seeing God's hand, I have geese. The fact that God sends geese was confirmed for me one day. Picture this. I am at home, and I hear the geese. I hurry outside to my front yard. I see geese flying, but they have already passed over my house. Another group of them flies over my neighbor's backyard. Now a V of geese, honking and flapping its way, is coming toward the air space over my house. The V-formation flies overhead along my property line as though it will fly straight over my backyard and keep going that way, but instead, it changes direction when it gets to my house. The entire formation, still honking, makes a right-angle turn away from the property line and flies over the length of my house. At the end of my house, it makes another ninety-degree turn and resumes its original direction of flight.

I felt wonderfully singled out. God is creative. And He is saying over and over to me and you, "I love you."

Who is God?

Then Moses said to God, "Behold, when I come to the Israelites and say to them, 'The God of your fathers (ancestors) has sent me to you,' and they say to me, 'What is His name?' What shall I say to them?" God said to Moses, "I Am who I Am"; and He said, "You shall say this to the Israelites, 'I Am has sent me to you.'"

Exodus 3:13–14 (AMP)

Trust His Heart

The sign on the church's front lawn said, "When you can't see God's hand, trust His heart." Let's imagine the sign sparked a conversation between two people going down the street in a car.

Son: Look, Dad! There's your answer!

Dad: What? What are you talking about?

Son: That sign back there said when you're having trouble, trust God.

Dad: What do you know about my troubles?

Son: I know you seem different, and you get mad at me a lot.

Dad: Well, that's because—no, you're right, son. It's grown-up stuff, and having no money, and—It'll be okay.

Son: Dad, why was mom crying last night?

Dad: So, what did that church sign say? Yes, it's like that. Your mom and I have prayed, and we haven't gotten any answers yet. Does God want us to move? Get another job? Sometimes it feels like life is happening too fast. I'm getting old too quickly. Enjoy your youth, son.

Son: Dad, you're not old. I have teachers a lot older than you, and they're still going strong.

Dad: (chuckling) You're right, son. I still have plenty of good years in me yet. It's like that sign says, "When you can't see God at work in your life, trust His love for you." I can do that.

Dear Reader,

Do you sometimes feel like this dad? Like you are looking for answers and getting frustrated? I appreciate Oak Park Community Church of God in Salem for their sign. It gives an encouraging word. I may not have the answers to all my questions, but I know God's heart.

His heart is love. We have examples of His love. The Amish community who suffered the tragedy of a gunman entering their schoolhouse and killing their children reached out to that gunman's widow with loving support. They extended love to her in the name of God, who tells us to forgive each other.

On an international level and in the name of Jesus, Samaritan's Purse gives spiritual and physical aid to victims of war, poverty, natural disaster, and disease. They provide food, clothing, shelter, programs, and medical supplies because God tells us to rescue those who are hurting.

An example closer to home is Love In the Name of Christ (Love INC), coming to Woodburn in the Fall. Their mission statement says, "Following Jesus Christ, who transforms lives, we equip our community to love, serve and connect with dignity."[4]

I remember an incident when God's love was tangible to me. I was single at the time, grieving my divorce. I was sitting on the floor of my studio apartment, watching television. When a love scene came on, I felt alone and sad. I thought, *I wish someone would love me like that.* In answer, I heard inside myself, "I love you." I didn't hear it with my ears. There was no one else around. No one there but me and Jesus. Hallelujah.

I believe you have examples of God's love in your life too. God doesn't just give to one person and not give to others. His love is for everyone. The question is, when can you grab some minutes today to remember God's love toward you? I invite you to think about His love. Think about His goodness.

June 2008

God, Our Loving Father

God ran. He wasn't in the Olympics. There wasn't an emergency that took Him by surprise and needed His attention. He wasn't running to get His exercise. In a story Jesus told to show God's love for us, He says, "While he was still a long way off, his father saw him and was filled with compassion for him; he ran to his son, threw his arms around him and kissed him" (Luke 15:20, NIV).

The story is of a child who got restless at home. He didn't want to wait until his dad died to get his inheritance. He wanted his money right away, so his dad gave it to him. He left home and spent all his money until he had nothing left but an empty stomach and a new appreciation for how good his father had been to him. When the child comes to his senses, he feels bad. He decides to apologize to his dad. He hopes his dad will let him come back and work as a servant in his former home. The dad in Jesus' story does much more than that. The dad has been watching, longing for his child's return. When he sees his son off in the distance, he takes off running to meet him.

This story from the Gospel of Luke shows us the measure of God's love for us. When we go toward God, His arms are open wide to us. He has treasures to share with us. He rejoices to see us. We make Him happy.

This God who loves us with such exuberance is the same God whom Isaiah saw in a vision.

> I saw the Lord seated on a throne, high and exalted, and the train of his robe filled the temple. Above him were seraphs, each with six wings: With two wings they covered their faces, with two they covered their feet, and with two they were flying. And they were calling to one another: 'Holy, holy, holy is the Lord Almighty; the whole earth is full of his glory.' At the sound of their voices the doorposts and thresholds shook and the temple was filled with smoke.
>
> Isaiah 6:1–4 (NIV)

God is awesome. He could just sit back on His throne and receive praises all day, but instead, He longs for us. He looks for us so that He can give us love, mercy, beauty, and joy. I am grateful for these descriptions of God: God the magnificent and God the loving father. When I think about God in His magnificence and His being my father, I feel my love for Him. I fall in love with Him over and over again. When I think about who He is, it's like I'm looking at Him, and I get happy, even giggly. What does love feel like to you? When you contemplate the one you love, do you feel secure? Calm? Joyful? I feel all these things when I sit and look at God.

It seems to me God feels some of this way too. A friend sent me an email. I've changed some details to preserve privacy. My friend is a single mom, and Harold is her son. Here's the email:

I had a 'good' God experience (not that there's any bad ones) a couple of days ago on my break and wanted to tell you about it. There was only one spot left in business class Harold needed to take and he had to get a lot of paperwork together in order to register. I prayed for the Lord to leave the spot open, and he did. Then on my break, I was praying and grateful and was thinking about how I wish I had a husband to share these proud-type feelings with and how my ex was missing out on so much by not seeing how great Harold is. The Lord told me He shares my same feeling about Harold and how He is his Dad. It was better than the way I'm wording it, but it was a great experience, which I was able to share with Harold.

Did you know that God is available to protect the widow and father the fatherless? He said so centuries ago, and He is still saying it (Psalm 68:5). He hasn't changed. You can trust Him to be a faithful, loving husband and father.

October 2008

Truth about God

"Are you lying to me?" If you ask someone who lies that question, you won't know whether to believe them or not. Their answer could be a lie. If you ask me that question, I will tell you why you can believe me. You can believe me because:

1. You know me. You can look at my monthly columns, written over the last twenty months, and get an idea of who I am. I've shared with you my family, my thoughts and feelings, my intimacies with God.

2. I am not trying to sell you anything. I am not in your face asking you to give me anything in return for what I'm writing. Because I'm not selling you anything, I do not have to lie to make what I'm offering more appealing to you. There's no need for me to exaggerate, gloss over, or tell you less than the whole truth.

The point I want to make is twofold. Column after column, I'm telling you the truth. You can believe it when I tell you God is real and He cares for you personally and specifically.

Also, you can respond with openness to what I'm writing. I'm not calling you at dinnertime to tell you your car warranty is about to expire. When I tell you that God is real and He cares for you, you can let that truth sit in front of you. Then you can let God's love for you get under your skin. You can relax your defenses because no one is there for you to defend yourself against. It's just you and the words on the page.

The way I know about God's love is that I've been a Christian for almost forty years. During these decades, I have worked as a church secretary, attended church services and conferences, and enjoyed a one-on-one relationship with God who loves me. What I mean is: a church secretary does not just answer the phone and use the computer. As secretary, I led a Bible study, prayed with and informally counseled people. I saw up close the lives of men and women who had dedicated their lives to God. I saw the evidence in their lives of God's goodness and faithfulness.

The years of church services and conferences educated and enlightened me. They have nurtured my relationship with God, who loves me.

It almost seems like that should be His name: *God Who Loves Me*. He is close. It's like He is holding my hand. It's like He highlights Bible verses for me so that when I read my Bible, the verses catch my attention and touch me. It's like when He wants me to do something, that thing keeps popping into my consciousness until I do it. If I've gone off on my own tangent of activity, even with good intentions, then I abruptly lose interest in the activity. If it's not something God has for me to do, it's like a balloon popping. Suddenly, no more drive. Sometimes, He says yes to my requests. Sometimes he says no. His *no* is gentle, though. He has my best interest at heart, and I trust Him.

Some mornings I wake up with a song in my heart. I receive those songs as being gifts from God. I am careful not to treat God as my personal butler or gofer because, after all, He is the creator of the universe, but I do go to Him with all my requests. I need help with everything from finding lost things to figuring out how to raise a teenager. That's what being in a relationship with *God Who Loves Me* is like for me. When I get too busy or distracted to notice *God Who Loves Me*, I start to feel lonely, hungry, empty.

I felt empty before I met Jesus for the first time. Sometimes, when I've gone days without praying or reading my Bible, I get some of that feeling again. I don't like it. It wakes me up, and I go back to my one-on-one with Him.

All of this is the truth. God bless you.

December 2008

Reasoning about Jesus

My mom wants to help you. She helps lots of people. She makes care packages for her local domestic violence shelter. She has produced countless lap blankets for persons needing a touch of warmth and comfort. Now she asked me to help you. Someone told her that Jesus was not born in the middle of winter. When she asked me about it, I acknowledged Jesus was probably born earlier than we celebrate His birth. For generations and around the globe, we've been observing Jesus' birth later in the year than the Bible says it happened. It's not the Bible's fault. The reasoning behind this assertion has to do with clues internal to His birth story.

Little details can say a lot. For example, there's a story in Joshua that mentions a river being at flood stage all during harvest time. Earlier in the story, it had mentioned a woman having stalks of flax laid out on her roof. The flax would only have been laid out at harvest time. The two details confirm each other.

In the story of Jesus' birth, there's the detail of the shepherds tending their flocks. The angels come to tell them the wonderful news: a savior has been born! What some notice is shepherds would not be tending sheep in the winter. Tending sheep in the fields is a late summer/fall job. I've heard that before, and I think it's interesting. It need not be faith-shaking, though. The bottom line is we need a savior, and one has come. That's what I told my mom, and that's what she asked me to tell you.

If you need any assurance that Jesus' birth was worthy of the angelic announcement and worthy of celebrating whenever that celebration occurs, then please note the following: Jesus fulfilled prophecies with His birth. More than four hundred years before He was born, men of God divinely predicted His family line, the timing of His birth, how He would be born, what His name would be, where He'd be born, and that kings would bring him gifts. With His birth, these prophecies were fulfilled. Specifically, detail-wise fulfilled. He was born when, where, and how He was supposed to be.

As a mere man, Jesus could not have engineered His birth to fulfill these prophecies. There has to be some other explanation for how Jesus fulfilled these and more than fifty other prophecies concerning His life, death, and life after death.

What do you think?

There's another detail I want to share with you. It's a personal favorite. In the culture of Jesus' day, there were servants who waited on their master as he ate his meal. If the eating man got up from his meal, there were two ways he could position his napkin. If he left his napkin unfolded, that meant he had finished his meal and the servant could clear the dishes away. If he folded his napkin, that told the servant to leave the meal in place. The master was coming back. Keep that cultural tidbit in mind, please, and note what the Bible says about Jesus' rising from the dead. In the Gospel of John (20:6–7, RSV), it says Simon Peter "Went into the tomb; He saw the linen cloths lying, and the napkin, which had been on his head, not lying with the linen clothes but rolled up in a place by itself."

Dear Reader, Jesus is alive after being dead, and He left His face cloth folded up. He's coming back! Praise God! If He doesn't return within the next sixteen days, Merry Christmas to you. God be with you.

December 2009

The Day, God, You Are Good

The first thing a person notices upon meeting Ewart Brown is his friendliness. He is outgoing. Then, one notices his friendliness is inclusive. It's community-building. He unites the people he is with. His manner draws people in and connects them. I was curious how he does it and if he does it on purpose. I asked him.

Suzanne: Ewart, I'm going to introduce you to my readers by telling them you are a retired pastor from East Salem Adventist Church and currently available as a mediator. You have been married to the same woman for almost forty years. You live and are active in the Woodburn community. Is there anything you'd like to add to this?

Ewart: Yes. As a mediator, I build positive relationships. That's the aim of my business. I do it in business and home settings. I teach *Affirmation Comebacks*. The goal is to do away with negatives, accusations, and criticisms and be fluent with affirmations and encouragements. Also, I was an administrative pastor for ten years and pastored for more than thirty years total. I spent most of those years here in the Northwest. And the three most important things to me are my connection to God, connection with my family and working to help the people of Woodburn see the value in each other and build relationships with each other.

Suzanne: I'm interested in the spiritual markers in your life. Would you tell me about your spiritual development?

Ewart: Yes. At age 12, I first became interested in church life. *Church life* was reading the Bible, going to church, and being good. The truth was, I didn't know anything else. Around eighteen or nineteen years old, I had the first encounter that gave me real knowledge that someone was at the center of church life. I discovered that what was really important was a relationship with Him. Those times were so precious.

I had a one-on-one relationship with God. I just enjoyed being with Him. In Jamaica, I would go into the woods just to sit and talk with God. He and I together. At this time, my intimate times with God were very emotional. The relationship had a lot of feelings attached to it, sometimes to the point of tears. Later, when I started to prepare for ministry and pastoring, there was a shift in this because I was involved with caring for others. I was not as available to take care of my own intimate needs with God. My relationship was, therefore, less emotional.

Now that I am retired, my focus has expanded, and I have a different understanding of intimacy with God. It's less emotional and less tied to the practices of Bible reading and prayer. Those are good practices, and I'm not saying anything against them—

Suzanne: You still do those practices?

Ewart: Yes. And what I'm discovering is that I am also spending time with God when I am with those who love Him. When I am with those He loves, I am happy. It's like being with Him. I am no longer alone doing the disciplines, but I am enjoying God in the midst of being with His people. The church is bigger than the church building. God is in the world where His children are.

My greatest joy is that God is wherever His people are. For example, when there's a Mexican fiesta, God is there. When children are playing together, God is there. When I am holding a baby in Safeway, God is there. That makes me free to find God everywhere.

Suzanne: I can see the freedom you describe in how you relate to people. Now I have a better understanding of your outgoing manner: it's rooted in your knowing God's presence moment to moment. Thank you for sharing, Ewart.

Ewart: You're welcome. Tell your readers, the day is good. God is good. You are good.

August 2010

God Still Communicates Today

My son asked me, "What does God's voice sound like?" Over time, Dillon has heard me say, "God told me," and "If I'm hearing correctly, God seems to be saying—" Therefore, one day, Dillon asked me about God's voice. I answered Dillon, and now I'd like to add to my answer. It's such a good question.

The first time I heard God's voice, I heard it inside myself. My ears didn't hear it. I heard it in my gut. He said three words, and I heard it as seven words. He said three words, and I heard, "It is okay. It will be okay." I was in a stressful situation and was greatly comforted by what I knew was God's voice. No one had to tell me it was God. The voice was self-identifying. I just knew. I didn't note the pitch or accent of the voice. The experience was one of surprise, comfort, and being thrilled that God speaks.

I tell Dillon he can learn to recognize God's voice as he reads his Bible. That's what happened to me. When I was a younger Christian, about thirty years ago, I was reading about John the Baptist when I got caught by the part that says, "Prepare the way for the Lord, make straight paths for him" (Mark 1:3, NIV). I didn't realize I was stuck until I noticed I just kept re-reading that line, like a record or a CD with a skip. When I discovered I couldn't get beyond that sentence, I realized God was speaking to me. His voice, while not audible, was still directed at me personally. He meant for me to perceive His request.

I appreciate God's creativity and persistence in communicating with me. There was a season in my life when I was battling a certain sin. First, God used my conscience to tell me, over and over, to stop sinning. When I didn't stop, God used a dream and scripture to get my attention. In the dream, I am sitting down at the end of a long, narrow, dimly-lit, empty hallway. Then it gets horrible. Stuff starts falling on my head. I knew what the stuff was, but I will leave that to the imagination.

Within the next couple of days, I came across a scripture in the Old Testament in which God was speaking to some disobedient people. He told them He was going to "spread on your faces the offal from your festival sacrifices" (Malachi 2:3, NIV). It was a matter of being disgraced. Yes, God can be quite graphic at times!

I believe God desires a relationship with us so much that He pursues us. He's courting us. Sometimes He will say the same thing in different ways over three days. After getting the same message over and over, I finally get it: God's speaking!

To illustrate: I will be thinking about some aspect of my relationship with God. For example, to mature, I need to let go of my fear and trust God more. I will be experiencing an inner tug of war between my allegiance to fear and my allegiance to God. Within days, I will hear this topic mentioned in church, receive a Christian newsletter about the issue, and open a book at random and find the encouragement I need to let go of fear and trust more. When life happens with such connectedness, I hear God's voice.

God uses other people to speak to us. Numerous times, I have turned on the Christian television channel just in time to hear the person speak exactly the word I needed to hear at that moment. God is speaking with the aid of the person on the television. His voice is sometimes as quiet as the prompting to turn on the Christian channel.

I have somewhat come to recognize God's quiet voice. I have to say *somewhat* because there are times when He tells me to do something, and I don't do it because I think it's just me. I find out after I don't do it that it was God. I regret those instances of my deafness.

Lately, God is using His quiet voice with me. I don't mind. It still thrills me to know that God speaks. I am still comforted and encouraged to receive from Him. After all, if we want to hear God's voice loud and clear, we have only to look at the cross where Jesus hung and then consider the empty tomb.

September 2010

Proof of God in My House

I got proof recently that God was at my house.

One Saturday morning, my husband, Gilbert, was taking an online class. Passing the classes is important. While they are advancing him toward his goal of full-time ministry, they cost money and time. Each class, taught by a different church leader, still has the same overall structure. Class time is 8:00 a.m. to 12:00 p.m., two consecutive Saturdays. There is assigned reading. The homework's due date is usually a week after the last class. But not this class. The teacher said the homework was due before the day's end.

Gilbert was already tired. Then he received a call for help. A client had water line problems. Gilbert had to go to work. It was not a situation where he could say, "Call someone else, please." We picked up PVC pipe at a hardware store. Next stop: the bank. At 2:30 p.m., we were at the client's house. After surveying the problem, we went again to a store for a smaller pipe. It was then Gilbert realized he'd left his debit card in the ATM at the bank. At this point, I noticed how calmly Gilbert was continuing to do the next thing in front of him. He called the bank to cancel his debit card. I credit his calmness to prayer. At the first store, I had sent a text to a friend to please pray. Our friend responded, "I prayed, and I heard it will work out." I was reassured and grateful.

We got home around 5:00 p.m. I helped as much as ethically allowable. I gave Gilbert the structure of the paper. He did the research, soul searching, and writing. I typed and sent the paper to his teacher.

After dinner, I text our praying friend:

Me: It all worked out. God is good.

Friend: Was he done by 7:30? Thanks for letting me pray.

Me: Final act of a long day, his homework emailed to the teacher at 7:50 p.m. What did you experience?

Friend: I prayed again about 7:30 and got that he was close but not done. That he wouldn't be up late doing it. God is good.

Dear Reader,

God could only know Gilbert was close to being done if God was there, in our house with us. Ever since, I have been rejoicing that God is right here with me. Praise God. He redeemed a day of spiritual attack. God lives in you. God is with you. No matter what. Always. Tell your heart.

October 2018

A Love Message from God

I got to the Bible study a little early but still was surprised that no one else was there yet. For the entire year, I had never been the first one to arrive at the church. I figured someone was around somewhere in the church because there were cars in the parking lot, and the church door did open when I turned the doorknob, but there was no one in the fellowship hall where the Bible study was going to be.

While I waited for others to show up, I looked around the room. I saw a table toward the back of the room and walked over. It was the middle of December, so I was not surprised to see a tall bag of Christmas ornaments on the table. I started taking them out of the bag, admiring their color and sparkle. There was a blue ornament ball and a fancy silver ball, but then I saw the red one. It was true red with red sparkles on it. It was the most beautiful of all the ornaments and quite possibly the prettiest ornament I had ever seen. It captivated me. And then I heard God say to my spirit, "As beautiful as this is, you are even more beautiful to me."

A love message from God that I want you to hear for yourself too. You are beautiful to God. He made you, He loves you, and His love is true. You are His true love.

.

God-Given Prayer

There is reason to hope. God has provided all we need to get through this. I will explain. I was thrilled to find the book, *The Priestly Prayer of the Blessing: The Ancient Secret of the Only Prayer in the Bible Written by God Himself.* In his introduction, author Warren Marcus says,

> This book introduces the reader to a new and life-changing relationship with the heavenly Father as He makes Himself available to us in a way that's tangible. I believe this is the time when the heavenly Father is going to make Himself known to the church in a way like never before.[5]

That fits what God has shown me: His love for us is deep and immense and right in front of our faces. I imagine God's Spirit pouring this encouraging insight upon us. This is God's current events, from of old. News and social media say their points, but God is the beginning and the end. He has always said He loves us and will take care of us.

We've known for years the richness of Psalm 91. Any catastrophe that could happen is covered with God's promise of safety and rescue. All He asks is that we go to Him and hang on to Him as if we are attached with super glue.

Now see Numbers 6:24–27, by which God wants to claim ownership of and responsibility for us. I've known this prayer for years and just discovered the Hebrew understanding - the visuals that go along with the English words in our Bibles. Listen up! I know God's presence when I pronounce these truths over myself. Numbers 6:23 says God wants His children to declare these truths. Since God wants to bless us, let's be obedient and ask Him to bless us.

Here's the Hebrew understanding.[6] Say it out loud. I've personalized it so you can claim it for yourself.

May my Heavenly Father, (He who exists), kneel before me making Himself available to me (like a good father kneeling before his child) in order to minister and bestow His gifts and promises.

May my Heavenly Father, (He who exists), guard me with a hedge of thorny protection that will prevent Satan and all my enemies from harming my body, soul, mind and spirit, my loved ones and all my possessions.

May my Heavenly Father, (He who exists), illuminate the wholeness of His being toward me - continually bringing me to order so that I will fulfill my God-given destiny and purpose.

May my Heavenly Father, (He who exists), provide me with perfect love and fellowship - never leaving me - and give me sustenance, provision and friendship.

May my Heavenly Father, (He who exists), lift up and carry His fullness of being toward me (bringing everything that He is to my aid) supporting me with His divine embrace and His entire being.

May my Heavenly Father, (He who exists), set in place all I need to be whole and complete so I can walk in victory, moment by moment, by the power of the Holy Spirit. May He give me supernatural health, supernatural peace, welfare, safety, soundness, tranquility, prosperity, perfection, fullness, rest, harmony, as well as the absence of agitation and discord.

Numbers 6:22-27

Marcus has written a 221-page book on this prayer, but I am limited here. His website is www.warrenmarcus.com.

God has provided for you by offering you His entire self. Everything that God has belongs to you if everything you have (including your life) belongs to Him. What a wonderful trade!

July 2020

The Good News

For God so [greatly] loved *and* dearly prized the world, that He [even] gave His [One and] only begotten Son, so that whoever believes *and* trusts in Him [as Savior] shall not perish, but have eternal life.

John 3:16 (AMP)

Where Is God?

Where is God? Right now, while you are reading this, where is He? Of course, He is right there with you. Because God is everywhere, He is there. He's not like a watchmaker who set a watch to ticking and then put it on the shelf to fend for itself. God is everywhere. That's the easy answer to my question.

However, I am not looking for an easy answer. I am looking for that place in you where this question can live. I invite you to carry this question through your day and occasionally answer it. For example, have you ever heard of *migas*? It's a Texan breakfast dish consisting of eggs scrambled with fried tortilla bits and melted cheese. You can add onions and garlic for increased flavor, but it is delicious and rich just as it is. Last Saturday, I was eating migas when I considered the question, "Where is God?" It was not hard to answer the question because the migas tasted so good. I answered myself, "God is right here. He provided me my favorite meal."

It was not as easy to answer the question later when I was in the middle of a very emotional discussion with a family member. The question occurred to me, but I was being tossed around in a sea of emotions. I could not rejoice in God's closeness. I had only my faith to reassure me that He was still close by. Sometimes life is like that.

One Sunday, singing love songs to God, His presence was almost physically palpable. I started to cry with love. I had to stop singing for a minute because I was part of a trio singing in front of everyone. It just would not have been conducive to everyone's worship of God to have me break down and start crying!

Monday night, I'm wondering about you, reader. What are the ways you use to remind yourself of the spiritual? Do you have a favorite scripture? Do you take breaks in your day for prayer and reading? This is what I wonder: are you as close to God as you want to be? If not, can I share with you a few more things? God is. He exists. When God spoke with Moses, God said, "I am" (Exodus

3:14) Moses believed. He saw that the bush was on fire, but it was not burning up.

Someone may tell you we all arrived here via evolution. I have problems with the theory of evolution. It cannot explain the existence of something as intricate as an eyeball or a human hand. Also, where did we get our sense of justice and fair play if there is no *one who is just*?

God is as close as your heartbeat. When I first tried out God, I told Him, "God, if you are there, I need you. Come into my life, my heart. Forgive me my sins." I was not sure if God existed, but He did, and He does. He answered my prayer, and that is a *good* thing!

I invite you to ask yourself some questions: Does God exist? Where is God? The next question for you I present with love. If you say there is no God, this last question is for you. Here it comes. I believe in a loving God who invites me to share eternity with Him in heaven. If I'm wrong, and after death, there's nothing, then I will never know it. After death, I'm dead. On the other hand, if you believe there's nothing after death, what happens if you are wrong? Are you willing to take that risk?

Please remember what I have said. God is as close as your heartbeat.

February 2008

God Wants to Be Found

Am I a crazy person? Crazy people hear voices, and I hear a voice. The first time was about thirty years ago. I was working, washing dishes in a coffeehouse. I heard a voice say, "It is okay. It will be okay." There was no one around. I heard it inside myself, just below my lungs. I only heard three syllables, but they conveyed the meaning of the seven words. I was surprised and comforted.

These days, I still hear the voice, but it's much quieter. It's like a whispered thought in my head. I have to be quiet to hear it. It's still the same voice.

It is hard to explain, but I tell you, the voice is self-identifying. Even the first time I heard Him, I knew it was God. No one had ever told me God still speaks today. I wasn't asking God to speak to me. But there was no question nor doubt. Maybe because by then, I'd already been reading the Bible for about a decade. Maybe I recognized the audible voice because I knew the written voice. When I read emails, I hear the person's voice that sent me the email. While reading their words, I imaginatively add their voice. Maybe it was like that only in reverse.

Or maybe it was a God thing.

When I believe in God, am I deluded? When I pray about my fears and worries and feel consoled, is that coincidence? When I prayed for my sister-in-law's hurt finger, and the pain immediately went away, was that hypnosis?

There's a joke about a man looking for a parking space. He needed one so badly that he even prayed and promised he would go to church the following Sunday if God gave him a parking space. Just then, a space opened up. The man concluded his prayer with, "Never mind. I found one."

If I'm deluded, there are a lot of people deluded along with me. We could call it a worldwide epidemic. It's a strong delusion too, people have even died for it. Is it the Buddhists who say life is an illusion? What if the illusion is that life is an illusion? What if it's not insanity nor an illusion? What if God is real? If God is real, then my faith is valid. That's a big deal.

With the confidence that my faith is well-placed, I can express my thanks and appreciation to God, who gives me an afternoon's golden light on the trees and the joy of geese flying overhead. When I know that I know that God is real, then I begin to realize that He's calling me to trust Him more, but that is not all. Are you wondering about God or your life? Are you worried about your future or your present? If so, please note that the best part about God's being real is His promises to us are real. His promise to all who wholeheartedly search for Him is that He will be found (from the 29th chapter of Jeremiah).

I agree with an email I read the other day. It said, "The evidence of God's presence far outweighs the proof of His absence."[7] I invite you to act a little crazy. Seek God. He wants to be found.

April 2009

Jesus Saves

I have two confessions to make. The first is that I was terrified. My soul shook at the thought of death. Someday, we are all going to die. My second confession is that I have tried to protect others from that terror, which is gut-churning and blinding. Now I see that my desire to protect others was short-term thinking and hypocritical. If today I wish you well while ignoring the possibility of your tomorrow, then how sincere is my love for you?

I wish upon no one the terror of seeing hell. I don't want to look. You probably don't want to look either, but it exists. Just as sure as there is a list of commandments, there is a consequence for breaking them. The same God who gave us a conscience says each person will face judgment after death.

You know God does what He says He will do. For over two years, I have been sharing with you my experiences and knowledge of God's faithfulness and power. My goal has been to encourage you with tales of God's care and closeness. For over thirty-five years, God has been good to me. I have more stories to tell you. But talking about God's love is incomplete when you don't know why it's so important that we have an ongoing relationship with Him. I have to tell you this stuff. If I didn't tell you, it would be like I saw you headed straight into a disaster, and I kept my mouth shut. How cold would that be?

Consider this, please: God is multi-faceted. Because He is justice, He cannot let sin go unpunished. Since the beginning, sin has always led to death. But, hallelujah, God is not only justice. He is also love. When Jesus was here, He demonstrated what God is like: compassionate, loving, and having authority over evil. It would have been a blessing if He could have stayed among us. Why did He have to die on a cross? Why couldn't He at least have lived a long life and died in His sleep?

You probably have heard it said that Jesus saves. Has anyone ever explained why we need saving? Has anyone ever told you that to break one of the commandments is enough to bring on the consequence of sin and hell? Ouch! If I were a swearing person, now would be when I would use a few choice words. This is hard news to deliver, but there is a way we can escape this heated trajectory.

Sin brings death. Therefore, Jesus agreed to die. Justice required death, so love took the blow for us. Jesus then demonstrated His authority over evil. He didn't stay dead! Again, hallelujah. Do you believe what I'm telling you? If not, check it out. Ask someone who knows Jesus. If you believe me, acknowledge your sin and the danger you're in. Ask Jesus to save you. Don't lose out on the lasting benefits of God's love. I urge you: don't say *someday* to His offer of salvation. Have peace with me. Do what you have to do, so on judgment day, you can say, "Jesus saves me."

June 2009

Friendship with God

I still consider her my friend, even though she has made it clear she doesn't want to communicate with me anymore. We did the things friends do, shared our secrets, prayed for each other, and helped each other for about five years, and then she stopped answering my calls and wouldn't return my messages. I'm not sure why. Maybe it was because I was getting into a family crisis which she didn't want to go into with me. It might have hit her too close to home. I may never know. I still hope to hear from her, but it's been more than four years since she cut me off. I'm not sitting by the phone.

In contrast, I have four friends who have been my friends for decades. I don't like the philosophy that says we have some friends for a reason and some for a season. I have experienced the truth of that philosophy, but I still don't like it. I want to make friends and have those friends for life. Even if I don't phone or email my old friends Bonnie, Alison, Karen, or Anne for months at a time, when I do contact them, we pick up right where we left off. Our hearts are still open to each other.

It looks like the heart is the key to this question of how to keep a friendship. Over the decades, my friends and my lives have included marriages, children, divorces, illness, career advancements, and everything else life holds. But our friendship is not based on our marital status or careers. We started out connecting through our commonality, but now we stay connected through our love for each other.

That's how it is with Jesus, too. When He was here as a man, He connected with us on our human level. He ate, walked, slept, and laughed with us. He came. He connected with us. And even though He left, we're still connected heart to heart. Before He left, He said He would no longer be visible to everyone but that He would be in our hearts.

The way I experience Jesus living in my heart is through our communicating. The other day I was feeling overwhelmed, and I laid it all out there. I told God about each one of my friends and family members who needed help. Their needs include marital healing, healing in the body, and employment. I felt like it was too much for me, and then I felt a renewal of my peace when the thought entered my head that God is big enough to handle it all. That reminder that God can handle it all was God-given. I can only assure you and ask you to believe that I did not answer my own feelings of discouragement. God spoke encouragement into me. I experienced it as a thought that I am confident was not self-generated.

Is God speaking to you? Are you speaking to Him? Is your heart open? If you need an introduction, please allow me: His name is Jesus. He's my friend for life. He wants to be your friend for life too.

October 2009

God Wants Us

The one thing I've observed in politics is that soon after the president publicly supports one of his people, that person is out of government office. Usually, the person is accused of some wrongdoing, and the president makes a statement on their behalf. Then, they are out of office and, the news is reporting the name of their replacement. I'm not analyzing this or pretending to understand it. It takes time to understand politics. I prefer to spend my time in other ways. Sometimes I think I understand spirituality.

I've invested a lot of time and energy in studying God. Naturally, I have felt like I knew God's bottom line. God's bottom line: we are not good enough to reach God on our own. We need a way to reach Him. Therefore, God gave us Jesus as the way. But why does God go to such lengths? A lot of the time, we ignore Him. How does He have such a high tolerance for rejection? I know the creator and sustainer of life, God Almighty, could zap us all into oblivion and start over with new people. I'm not talking politics now. I'm talking about existence and non-existence. So, when we say that God isn't real and just a myth, why does He put up with us?

God wants an everlasting relationship with us. That's why He did all He did. That's why He does all He does. It makes me smile every time I think of it. God wants to be family and friends with us. He created me so we could get to know each other and walk around together, holding hands.

You may be thinking, what about all the dos and don'ts of Christianity? Yes, there are rules for this relationship with God, just as there are rules for any relationship. We must believe in, love, spend time with, and trust Jesus. Please note: we don't exist because God wanted to rule over someone. He's not a control freak. The rules exist to serve the relationship.

God has done a lot to prove He wants us. John 3:16 (RSV) says, "For God so loved the world that he gave his only Son that whoever believes in him will not perish but have eternal life." Seeing God's love for me delights me. It relaxes me. It makes my eyes tear up.

How awesome is it that God wants us? Sometimes it seems no one wants us. We may feel rejected by a potential employer. We may feel lonely for a friend to whom we can pour out our hearts. We may feel separated from our family if we live miles from them and didn't even get to see them for the holidays. Look! We can take heart. When we go to God, He always accepts us. He's available to hear our heartbeat. Right now, He's like that father who stands in the middle of the road straining to catch a glimpse of his child returning home.

God did what He did and does what He does because He loves us. And I love Him.

January 2010

God and His Love Are Real

We have treasures among us.

As a member of Victory Outreach Church, Gilbert Ybarra, a Woodburn resident, and businessman goes into the most dangerous parts of a city, those areas that one could describe as war zones. He searches out the drug addicts and gang members to tell them about the love and hope available in Jesus.

Gilbert has taken the good news of Jesus to the dark alleys of Sydney, Australia, and the violent parts of New York City. He's been as far south as the uneasy streets of Caracas, Venezuela, and, more locally, to the gang neighborhoods of northeast Gresham.

Gilbert and his fellow crusaders believe themselves sent out to share God's love. God's presence goes with them. Over the past sixteen years, he's been on thirty crusades. He continues to return home safe, even after being held up at gunpoint in Caracas.

Gilbert's life encourages me. I hope it will do the same for you.

Suzanne: Gilbert, I'm interested in the spiritual markers of your life. Besides your first encounter with God when you gave your life to Him, when have you felt closest to God?

Gilbert: First of all, I need to explain that crusades are a massive outreach to a city. For an evangelistic effort the size of a crusade, men, women, and youth come from all over the world to talk with people on the streets of that city. Along with this there is massive prayer and fasting before and during the crusade, and God's anointing comes. During a crusade, I feel His presence most evident. Preaching the gospel is the high point because the power is in God's Word.

Suzanne: Could you put into words what God is telling you at those times?

Gilbert: These are the people you need to reach.

Suzanne: Why do you think God sends you?

Gilbert: I've asked myself that question many times: "Why me, Lord?" Because God chooses the foolish things of the world. I thank God He chose me.

Suzanne: I recall that scripture that says, "For many are called, but few are chosen" (Matthew 22:14, LB). God calls many, but only some say yes to that call. What price have you had to pay to answer that call?

Gilbert: In a worldly way, the price is giving up a normal life. Every time I go out, I don't know if I'm coming back. We put our lives on the line. We do it because of our gratefulness. We're grateful to be alive.

Suzanne: It seems like gratefulness can be empowering. You can hold your fear at bay and go out with confidence. Where can a person get that gratefulness for themselves?

Gilbert: If you experience a long life of violence and drugs and you should be dead, and suddenly God rescues you from that lifestyle, it is like you owe your life to Him. I was a heroin addict for over twenty years, and God saved me. There's a scripture that says, "He who is forgiven much, loves much" (Luke 7:47, NIV). I think about all the times in my life I should have been dead. I survived drive-ups where the weapons of choice were tire irons, baseball bats, knives, and guns: a lifelong history of violence.

Suzanne: Remembering where you came from helps you to go forward. When that taxi driver in Caracas had a gun to your head, what helped you then?

Gilbert: My background is street-savvy. My street knowledge from my previous lifestyle.

Suzanne: What were you thinking?

Gilbert: I was thinking, *How am I going to get out of this? What's my move to overcome the enemy?*

Suzanne: What happened? What did you do?

Gilbert: I challenged him. He wanted my money and my belongings. I got out of the taxi and then challenged him to get out. He took off.

Suzanne: Have you asked God anything about this encounter?

Gilbert: I wonder if anyone else told him [the taxi driver] about Jesus after I told him. I wonder if he's in church.

Suzanne: You want something better for that taxi driver, don't you?

Gilbert: Yes, even though he held me up. I hope that what I told him before he held me up planted a seed for his life.

Suzanne: What do you want people to know about God?

Gilbert: That He's real and He's there waiting for you. He's there with open arms. Get to know Him. God's love is real.

June 2010

Can God Be Trusted?

Do you think God is asking us to trust Him more than we ever have? Is He telling us we can depend on Him? It seems that way to me. Because I want to trust God wholeheartedly, I went searching for proof of His reliability. In Psalms 13:5 (NIV), David tells God, "I trust in your unfailing love; my heart rejoices in your salvation." David knew God's protection, His forgiveness and the beauty of His love. It's obvious God moved in his life, but what about my life? Can God be trusted today?

I asked a couple of friends for their input. Specifically, I asked them if God had ever made them a promise and then let them down. I also asked, "What is the biggest thing you have ever trusted God for?"

Margo's Story of God's Unconditional Love

My friend, Margo, has been an active Christian for ten years. When I asked her if God had ever gone back on a promise, she said, "Heavens no. He's always come through." She elaborated about times when she's been crying and down on her knees. God gave her His peace. Also, at one time, she had a serious condition that was supposed to make her unable to have more children, but God healed her, and she did. Margo wants everyone to know that the only time she doesn't get what she needs is when she doesn't ask God for it.

I enjoyed hearing about God's faithfulness to Margo. She is a professional driver, and there have been times when cars have come so close to her on the road, she is sure angels are protecting her. Her daughter, son, and their spouses are all Christians. And they are raising their children to love Jesus. All of this is because of God working in their lives.

I want to underline something Margo told me: even at those times when Margo has been hurting and arguing with God, He's loved her. Sometimes I think I am not good enough for God to love me, but the biggest, best thing about God is He loves us no matter what. No matter if we are loveable or if we trust Him or not. I want to trust God more. Hence, this quest for assurance.

God's Way of Answering Sanford

I asked a friend, Sanford Washington, my questions about God. He's been a Christian for eighteen years. Sanford told me God has never let him down, but he has let himself down when he's prayed and expected God to do what he asked Him to do. He's now learned to listen for God's answer.

The biggest thing Sanford has trusted God for was his salvation. When he cried out to God that day, he knows God answered him because he began to do things he'd never done before. When Sanford told me this, I wondered if he meant he stopped certain behaviors. That wasn't it. When he reached out to God, he started speaking in tongues. This is not everyone's experience, but it showed Sanford that God heard and answered him. It was his turning point in believing that God is real.

Sanford made one final point that I found very helpful. To grow in trust, he reads his Bible. When he applies what he's read to his life, and things come through for him like the Bible says they will, it strengthens his belief system and trust.

I offer this to you as an invitation to try out what the Bible says. See if it's true.

November 2010

We All Need God's Love

"You could have been there." I was talking with my brother, and a couple of times, he said, "You could have been there."

We were talking about the Portland Christmas tree lighting and the thwarted bomb attempt. It's true. Any of us could have been there for the holiday tradition. Maybe you were there. Even before talking with my brother, I was emotional about the young Muslim's alleged goal. On the news, they reported a conversation between an undercover FBI agent and the 19-year-old Muslim. It went something like the FBI agent saying there would be many children at the lighting ceremony. The 19-year-old responded that is what he wanted. That response got me in my gut. You probably feel it too. Somehow, when an older person dies, they are a hero, and we mourn them, but when a child dies, we experience more grief because of the child's innocence. They have their whole life ahead of them.

I got some relief from this punch to my gut when my pastor mentioned the incident in Sunday's worship service. In an aside from his preaching, Pastor Max mentioned the young Muslim. He said if the FBI gave him to us, we would pray for him and bring him into our men's recovery home. We have recovery homes for persons wanting to get off drugs and alcohol. We offer the love of God to combat addictions. Pastor Max was not saying the young man has an addiction, but he needs God's love shown to him.

Pastor Max's point of view helped me. I could exhale and relax. Please join me in this perspective. No matter the person's style, color, addiction, frame of reference, or religion, we all need God's love shown to us. God is personally reaching out to Muslims.

From the website, *Breaking Christian News* on November 29, 2010:

> Tom Doyle, with a Christian ministry located in the Middle East, reports that the way people in the Middle East are coming to

Christ is amazing. He says, "We found that Muslim-background believers, many in our informal surveys—maybe even as many as half of them—had a dream or a vision before they came to Christ. They became a 'seeker,' found a believer, heard a message on the radio or found a Bible.

We'll ask people as we're talking. We'll say, 'Hey, we're Christians and you're Muslims, but there's this phenomenon happening about Muslims having dreams about Jesus. Do you know anybody? Have you had one?' We have met some people who have said, 'I did have a dream about Jesus, but I didn't know what it meant.' Then we go into the gospel."

According to a *Mission Network News* report, Doyle told the story of a woman in Egypt who stopped a Christian man on the street The woman said, "You are the one!" The Christian man didn't understand what she was talking about. She told him, "(In my dream) you were walking with me and Jesus, and you had that same striped shirt on, those glasses, those pants and those shoes. Jesus was telling me He loves me and wants to have a relationship with me!'

In her dream she reportedly asked Jesus, "What do I do?" In her dream Jesus told her, "Ask this man tomorrow when you see him."[8]

We cannot do any less than what God Himself is doing. We know that Jesus died to save, not condemn, the world. God knows who will accept and who will reject His offer of Jesus. God is the only one who knows. Since we don't know, we dare not judge who receives God's love and who does not.

God bless us, everyone.

December 2010

You Can Trust God

My thoughts resemble a crossword puzzle. I want to write about setting personal goals, living in the miraculous, Jesus and love, and several sentences about death. These subjects overlap and connect. Maybe their connections are not apparent to you yet.

First, let's get death out of the way. Recently, within eight days, three deaths happened near me. One of my in-laws died. Then the spiritual great-grandfather of Victory Outreach, David Wilkerson, was killed in a car crash. Finally, Osama bin Laden was killed. I'm thinking about the impact a life can have, about legacies, good and evil.

Pastor Dave Wilkerson is best known for the movie *Cross and the Switchblade*. God used him to reach New York City gang members with the good news of Jesus. He founded Teen Challenge. He was eighty years old and still pastoring. His church in Times Square, New York City, numbers 8,000. He is known in other countries for his work on behalf of orphans, the homeless, widows, and the struggling. His heart was evangelism. He used to write a newsletter. I would read each issue with eagerness to hear what he had to say and what God had revealed to him. He was a man of God, inside and out. His walk matched his talk. I will miss him.

Thinking about legacies reminds me of an item on my list of things to do. After I heard Brian Tracey at a conference talk about the power of goal setting, I decided to revisit my personal goals. Mr. Tracey gave us homework:

1. Write ten goals we want to accomplish in a year.
2. For each goal, write down everything we can do to achieve it.
3. Prioritize that list.
4. Ask ourselves, "What one skill do I need to reach my goal?"
5. Find someone who has that skill and learn from them.

Two of my goals are *living in the realm of the miraculous and sharing my love of Jesus with others*. When I reach these goals, I will impact the world and, someday, leave a good legacy. I could write a list of ways to achieve living in the realm of the miraculous. Perhaps a future column will include talking about the prayer of Jabez and saturating our minds with God's Word.

What I can't figure out is how to share with others my love for Jesus. If people could know how good He is, they would find it easier to love Him. We just had Easter, the most vivid portrayal of Jesus' love. And yet, the churches were not packed with crowds even outside straining to get in. I want to describe Jesus' love. He loves with big words and big promises. On the way to fulfilling all that bigness, He whispers encouragement and direction in my ear. I recently heard Jason Gray on the radio about his relationship with Jesus. He sang, "More like falling in love than something to believe in. More like losing my heart than giving my allegiance."[9] I agree.

Loving Jesus is the most personal thing I have. I've loved him for almost forty years so, there are layers of experiences and depth of love. I love him, and He loves me. This goes beyond my attempts to show you He is real. I want you to know you can trust him. If you talk to him, He will listen. If you read a Bible, He will speak to you through it. His voice is loving. His presence is peace.

I encourage you to tell Jesus you want to meet him. Pick up a Bible. Read the Gospel of John or Mark or read Romans. I promise you it will be the best thing you've ever done.

May 2011

What Do You Talk About?

One pre-Christmas afternoon, a friend and I went shopping at one of Salem's discount clothing stores. While my friend was looking for a little black dress, I was patiently waiting to go home. Meandering by a rack of sweaters, one caught my eye because it was so ugly. The color was too yellow to be green and too green to be yellow. It was a bright shade of no-you-can't-be-serious-about-anyone-buying-this-sweater. Still just looking for a way to pass the time, I noticed someone coming down the aisle who could join me in my disapproval of the offensive sweater.

I pointed out the sweater and asked, "Would this color look good on anyone?" She promptly replied, "I like that color." I feel embarrassed again as I am re-telling this incident. I had insulted this woman's sense of taste. Wanting to redeem the interchange some way, I noted the sweater's style was attractive. I politely fled the scene to find my friend, confess my faux pas, laugh at myself, to relieve my chagrin.

Thinking about it now, I wish I would have stayed to continue the conversation. The ice was already broken. Why not deepen the verbal connection? I could have asked what she thought about Obama's support of illegal immigrants or if she believed in the true reason for the season. Who is Jesus to her? Someone told me the other day she and her friend are different political parties. In fact, she said she doesn't talk to her friend about politics, religion, or money. I asked, "What else is there?" My question ended that conversation, so I would like to express the point here that we can talk about the changing weather, especially in Oregon. Still, if we want to leave behind our loneliness, connect with others, and positively impact this world, we need to be vulnerable with each other. Share ourselves.

It's true: we are not the same. But to have unity within our diversity, we need to express that diversity. Then we discover our points of agreement. We won't agree on everything, but we will be all right if we converse with love.

My thoughts come back to that question: What is the season's reason? Where do we find the personal acceptance we need to help us be vulnerable with each other? Are we afraid of each other? I believe we can be agents of healing for each other.

If we're not in love yet, can we start with tolerance for all and grow toward acceptance and appreciation? In the child's story, *Beauty and the Beast*, Beauty grows to love the Beast after she has interacted with and gotten to know him. In this land of the free, we are free to express ourselves. Free to love each other. Free to be gracious and helpful.

For me, Jesus is the one who undergirds my desire to be loving. He is how I can act graciously. His love is the way, truth, and life. How about you? Where do you stand?

December 2014

Creation Declares Goodness and Existence of God

How long does it take to start a movement? Rosa Parks unintentionally sparked one that quickly gained momentum. I have something much more modest in mind.

Woodburn is going to have an influx of visitors for the momentous August 21 celestial showing. It is estimated hundreds of thousands of people will be here. In the City of Woodburn's July 21 Eblast, we are advised to buy food, water, and gas ahead of time. I'm going to do that. No one likes waiting in long lines for groceries and gasoline. As a city, we have an opportunity to shine. The majority of our visitors have probably never been here. They might have even needed the internet to find us. And now they are coming.

When I came here from California looking for a new home, I traveled up and down Oregon. I settled in Woodburn because of the friendly people here. Over two decades later, I still think our town is a great place. Can we use our friendliness to make August 18–21 go smoothly for all of us? I suggest we treat each visitor with such courtesy that their smiling response will be, "Wow, Woodburn!" We will benefit because we will get to be the helpful, polite people we are. We all, citizens and visitors, will benefit as we focus on the positive. As we stand in line and stop at traffic lights together, we will need that positive focus.

As a Christian, I want to take this movement further. The presentation in the heavens is going to occur Monday morning. We will have Friday through Monday to meet and greet visitors. What I'm envisioning are mini-conversations all over town that point toward God. For example,

Visitor: Hi. Warm day today.

You: Yes, are you here for the show in the heavens?

Visitor: What? Yes, the eclipse.

You: Welcome to our town. We get some beautiful sunsets here too.

We have a broad horizon, and sometimes the colors are awe-inspiring. I just have to praise God!

I have learned from my evangelist husband, Gilbert, that any casual remark can lead to a mention of God. For instance, Gilbert had this exchange in a store last winter,

Man in line with him: It's cold today, but at least it's not raining.

Gilbert: We don't need any more rain!

Man: That's right. We're almost swimming now.

Gilbert: Yes, if we're going swimming, let's swim in the rivers of God's love.

We have our own giftings and styles. I admit I'm not an evangelist like Gilbert. I am trying to learn from him. Perhaps we could use these creative phrases when discussing the eclipse: God's hand at work, a show of divine creativity, a wonder in the heavens, a glorious marvel, an instance of the divine.

I'm not saying the eclipse is so special it deserves a movement. I am saying creation declares the goodness and existence of God. We can rightfully claim the grandeur and order of the universe is a display of God's glory. God is the one who made the sky, earth, sea, and everything in them. He does things to prove He is real. He shows us kindness, gives us rain and food, and fills our hearts with joy. God deserves a movement.

Why not use this opportunity to remind people there's hope in the world? Sometimes we need to be reminded. Will you join the movement?

August 2017

Love Heals

I had not seen my former husband, Stan, in over twenty years. I haven't even thought about visiting him until recently when I felt a nudge to check in. I discussed it with my now-and-forever husband, Gilbert. It felt like a God-nudge, so when I went down to Santa Barbara to visit my friend Alison, I asked her to call and ask Stan if it was okay to visit him.

There we were in Stan's living room: Alison, Stan, and I. I confessed I didn't know why I was there. Stan said, "It's okay." We talked. Stan's son went into the military, just like we always thought he would. I assured Stan I'm happy and well.

When it was time to leave, I asked if I could say a blessing over him. I have been impacted for months by Numbers 6:24–27. I recited,

> The Lord bless you and keep you; the Lord make his face shine upon you and be gracious to you; the Lord turn his face toward you and give you peace. So you will have on you the name of God's people and He will bless you.
>
> Numbers 6:24–27 (NIV)

Stan's eyes teared up and seeing this, my eyes teared. The moment was still and quiet. God was evident.

After leaving, Alison and I were quiet for a long time. Then we talked. It was good she shared the experience because she and I have been friends for over forty years. She knows me. It was even appropriate. She's been part of my life with Stan from the beginning. She was my maid of honor, wrote a song about our relationship, and even delivered the divorce papers to him. Now, she's witnessed the healing.

Of course, I do not know for certain why Stan's eyes almost spilled over. But I experienced healing of a wound I didn't know existed. To illustrate, here's a memory from our marriage: We are standing outside the back door, arguing about God. I want so desperately for

Stan to love Jesus. We argued about it a lot. I yell at him, "I'm *praying* for you!" He yells back, "I'm *praying* for you too!"

I was young and frustrated, but that's no excuse for badgering him about Jesus. The result of my nagging was pain. I wounded him and myself. I see that now, with the healing of my wound.

Sharing the blessing from Numbers was praying God's goodness upon him. It was a gift he could relate to because his heritage is Jewish. We shared a God moment. At that moment, I was healed. My hurt was soothed away.

Gilbert likes to sing that Tina Turner refrain, "What's love got to do, got to do with it?"[10] Then other times, he says, "It's all about love." It's very clear: Blessing someone brings God into the relationship. Sharing God's love brings healing. If we want to introduce someone to Jesus, it's all about love.

April 2019

Faith

For everyone born of God is victorious *and* overcomes the world; and this is the victory that has conquered and overcome the world—our [continuing, persistent] faith [in Jesus the Son of God]. Who is the one who is victorious *and* overcomes the world? It is the one who believes *and* recognized the fact that Jesus is the Son of God.

1 John 5:4–5 (AMP)

A Good, Loving, Forgiving God

I was not there, but could I please respond anyway? I want to say something to the woman in the Salem Wendy's who was questioning God.

Hello,

Your volume was loud enough that many heard your questions. I assume you did not mind others hearing you. I hope you do not mind my responding to you publicly. I understand one of your questions is, "Since God has not liked some people in the Bible, and I'm no different than those people, then why should I worship Him?" A friend of mine who was there in Wendy's said it seemed like you feel unworthy of God's love.

First, let me introduce myself. I've been a Christian for over thirty-five years. In high school, a Baptist pastor told me it didn't matter what denomination I belonged to as long as the denomination preached the Bible and Jesus as the Son of God who came in the flesh, died, and resurrected. That freed me to worship and serve in over eleven churches. I've been a deacon, Sunday school teacher, song leader, and secretary. I've not always been a goody-goody, though. There have been times in my fifty-two years that I have resisted God and taken over the reins of control. I'm not proud of those times. Thank goodness we have a forgiving God.

I am telling you this in the hopes you and I can connect. I don't know why you doubt your relationship with God, but I want to help you.

Enough of me. Are you feeling separated from God? My friend, who was in Wendy's when you were, told me you were quoting Scripture. It was obvious you know God and the Bible. Please remember: God loved the whole world and gave us His Son.

Let's look at a biblical character who started as a murderer and ended as a saint. Before he knew Jesus as Lord, Paul hunted down and killed Christians. He was there when the first Christian martyr, Stephen, was stoned to death. Acts 8:3 (NIV) says Paul was like a wild man, going everywhere to capture men and women and jail them. His mission in life was to kill Christians. Now, I'll say it again, thank goodness we have a forgiving God.

You know how mightily God used Paul. First, God got Paul's attention. Then Paul handed his life over to Jesus. Then God used him to establish churches, write almost half the New Testament, and leave behind a testimony that still offers hope today.

How different would the world be if Paul had not taken the good news of God's love to the Gentiles? What if Paul had not persevered through all his troubles? What if he had not had the attitude that his troubles were only momentary or had lost his focus on God?

God could use Paul because He and Paul were in a relationship. Paul said how much he valued God. He called his former life before he knew Jesus *trash*. He acknowledged God as his strength. He said

> I have been crucified with Christ and I no longer live, but Christ lives in me. The life I live in the body, I live by faith in the Son of God, who loved me and gave himself for me.
>
> Galatians 2:20 (NIV)

Is that what's happening with you, dear Wendy's customer? Is God asking you to give it up and give Him your all? I don't know. If that is what's happening, I trust that this is not the first time God has asked you to do something like this. My experience of God is that He prepares us before He asks for something. He loves on us and woos us. He gives us supports and encouragement. I invite you to look back and remember those divine gifts. They will give you the strength you need to go forward. We serve a good, loving, forgiving God.

May 2008

New Birth at Christmastime

Mine is an arranged marriage. I am thrilled that it is. If it had not been arranged, would I have met Gilbert? Let's see.

Three years before we met, I was a shy, goody-two-shoes type of person in love with someone else. Gilbert was a heroin addict. Then, God rescued Gilbert from a trash compactor. He was about to be compacted, but he cried out to the God he didn't even know yet, and the compactor stopped functioning. A few days later, Gilbert stumbled into a Victory Outreach recovery home.

While God was getting ahold of Gilbert and Gilbert was grabbing ahold of God, I talked to the man I loved about getting married. It was a very one-sided conversation. Gilbert traveled around the United States as an evangelist for over a year. God had delivered him from cigarettes, alcohol, and heroin. He was a new man: grateful and in love with Jesus. Gilbert was traveling, and I was stuck in one place. I tried to help my boyfriend see we were good together and should get married. The more I pushed, the quieter he got. I was getting nowhere but frustrated. Of course, I prayed. And God answered me. I didn't understand His answer, but sometimes life with God is like that. God said, "New birth at Christmastime."

One day in September 1995, I had lunch at Taco Time. They gave me a Christmas placemat. I wondered, "Why the Christmas theme in September?'" I heard inside myself, "New birth at Christmastime." After lunch, I got in my car, turned on the radio, and heard a man singing about a baby in a manger on Christmas morning. A Christmas song! Again, that inner voice, "New birth at Christmastime." Immediately, I went home to my studio apartment. I started asking God to confirm "New birth at Christmastime," and I heard a knock at my front door. It was my landlord. My studio was attached to his house. A woman there with my landlord introduced herself. She was an Avon lady, new to the neighborhood. She asked me if I would take a catalog. I looked at it. It was a Christmas catalog! That was all the confirmation I needed! God had answered my prayer before I could even finish it. From then on, I was waiting for Christmas to see what new birth was going to happen. It was hard to wait.

Before December, I broke up with my boyfriend. I gave up trying to convince him. In early December, Gilbert and I met when he walked into the Christian bookstore where I worked. I believe it was God that I was still working there. I had applied for work elsewhere but had not been hired. Thank goodness!

I saw right away Gilbert was easy to talk to. I invited him to the Bible study I attended. We kept talking and seeing each other. For Christmas, he invited me to his house. In January, he proposed. In March, we got married. Gilbert still travels as an evangelist. We minister together through our church. Indeed, the birth of a relationship, the birth of a new life, the birth of a grand adventure. Thank you, Lord.

September 2008

Have a God Day

If you know my friend Leslie, you have already heard about *Remnant*, and perhaps you were one of the forty people who got blessed there.

If you don't know about *Remnant*, please picture this scene: It's evening. You're in Yun Wah Chinese Restaurant's banquet room. You've already ordered, been served, and eaten your Chinese dinner. Maybe you had a cashew chicken dish. (That's my recommendation.) Then, the banquet of love and encouragement begins. With you are nearly forty of your friends. Some of them you've not seen in years, and yet you discover they are here tonight too. It's like a happy family reunion.

Leslie reserved the room for us. She invited everyone she knew. Not everyone could make it, but we're meeting again Friday, May 6, so hopefully then.

Leslie felt led by God to gather us and have a time of being together. It was God and all of us. The best part of the evening: God was there. God's presence could be felt. To me, being in God's presence feels like I am held in a loving hug. It's tangible power. The air is thick with His love.

When I feel God like that, sometimes I find myself giggling and smiling a lot. Sometimes I just want to be still and soak Him in. I want to stay close and never be far from Him. A pastor once told me, "When the presence of God is felt, the call of God is heard." There, in the banquet room of love, we heard and answered God's call to take action. We shared our personal stories. We prayed for each other. We prayed for you when we asked God for His blessings and His movement upon Woodburn, its churches and church people, and those who don't yet know Jesus. We covered everyone.

We had a good time singing songs, in English and Spanish. We worshipped God. We prayed in four languages: English, Spanish, Russian, and the heavenly language, tongues.

I've started a saying in my family and amongst my friends: "Have a God day." It's a shorthand way of saying, "Remember to focus on God today." Therefore, let me say it wasn't just a good time. It was a God time.

April 2011

It Wasn't Coincidence

Have you ever thrown a prayer upward, hoping someone was there to catch it? When the answer came, did you give someone credit, or did *coincidence* get the credit? Do miracles happen without our recognizing them? If it's a miracle that babies are born, and we woke up this morning, and the sun rises and sets every day, then we can be thankful for these events and work up our courage to believe in other miracles too.

I desire to live in the miraculous. My desire was born when I studied something Paul said to the Romans. He encouraged them to give their whole selves to God and be transformed by thinking new thoughts. What Paul said appeals because he said if we give ourselves wholly to God, we will know what God wants. In other words, don't just know about God. Don't just believe He is real. But everything we do, we do it for God. As we do things for God, He will lead us in what to do.

Let's put what Paul said with what Jesus said about those who have faith in Him will do greater works than He did. Jesus raised the dead, walked on water, and cast out demons. Jesus calls His followers to do great works. All this sounds like an invitation to live in the miraculous. Following God's lead into the miraculous requires a willingness to risk. One particular day, I had to risk wasting gasoline, looking foolish in the eyes of others, and feeling like I don't hear God right. I gained $8.69 worth of free gasoline, the joy of blessing a friend, and increased confidence that God is with me by taking those risks.

Are you wondering about the free gasoline? I was driving north to see a friend. Our time together was so important that I was petitioning God for success and strenuously praising His goodness. While involved in this active prayer and praise, I went for gas. I asked for $20 regular and handed over my credit card. Minutes later, I checked the pump and was surprised to see it at $23 and climbing.

I jumped out of my car and shouted, "I asked for $20 worth and it's at $25!" The attendants reacted calmly. They stopped the gasoline's flow. The charge was $28.69. They refunded me $8.69. I experienced that as a gift from God. Do you see it? I wasn't praying for free gasoline, but I was concerned that I was going quite a distance for a visit that might not even happen. If I didn't get to see my friend, that would be a waste of money.

What's even more important than free gas is after I found out the visit with my distant friend would have to be postponed, I turned home and asked God what I should do next. I felt gently nudged, mile by mile, to visit another friend. I dropped in to see this friend at her work. After we visited for a few moments, I felt God's nod to pray regarding our topic of conversation. We found a private place to pray together. We had a good time knowing God's presence and care.

God cares about our concerns. It is His pleasure to gift us. There's no such thing as coincidence. There is only God.

July 2011

We Believe

A song on the radio captures my attention every time it's on, "We believe in God the Father, and in Jesus Christ, His Son. We believe in the Holy Spirit. He's come to give us life. We believe in the crucifixion. We believe He conquered death. We believe in the resurrection and he's coming back again."[11] Yes! That is what we believe. Newsboys put our creed to music: music and truth to soothe wounds and lift spirits. I know you need soothing and lifting. Someone told me you did, and I trust Him.

I've not written lately because life has been full, but recently I felt an inner nudge to write a column. A few days after I felt the inner nudge, my husband Gilbert brought up the subject. He asked, "When are you going to write another column?" I can take a hint, but I was wondering what to share. I asked Gilbert, "What should I write about?" He reminded me we are living in crazy, sometimes scary times. As I prepared to write, that inner nudge was accompanied by Newsboys singing our creed.

We believe. Because we believe, we wake up, have peace, and are energized. For example, I experience bad dreams that seem so real that I have to work at shaking them off when I wake up. Last night, falling asleep, I asked God to protect me from those dreams and give me one of His dreams instead. This morning, I dreamt I was explaining the good news of Jesus to someone. In my dream, I said, "Jesus died on the cross because of me." Then I awoke.

It's a hard truth that my sin sent Jesus to the cross. I am remorseful and then grateful to Jesus. This morning's reminder of what Jesus did for me got me out of bed and got my house cleaner! I was full of energy! Thinking about what Jesus did for me, I could not just lie there snoozing. I wanted to get up and be happy around people. I wanted to share God with others.

I am glad you are part of my community, and we can all have the power of acknowledged truth. Is it true that:

* The Almighty is your daddy?
* God loves you with a rich and royal love?
* The creator and sustainer of all life lives inside you?
* Jesus wants you to have a wonderful life?
* Jesus would have accepted death even if you were the only one needing him to do it?
* Jesus did not stay dead?
* Jesus got the victory?
* Jesus is returning someday?

Since all of these are true, I invite you to think about them as if you were explaining them to someone else. Mull them over. Consider their ramifications. Say truth out loud and feel its power. And then enjoy the day God has set before you. He has plans to prosper you and to give you hope and a future.

October 2014

Respond with Love

Silly me. I saw people looking at their wristbands and thought watches were coming back. Then I learned people are not wearing watches but Fitbits that tell the time, their pulse, and how many steps they have taken that day. I am now wearing one. I started wearing a Fitbit for two reasons: my workplace gave me one, promoting its use by having monthly contests. October's contest prize was a $30 gift certificate to the movies. To win, I needed to average 8,000 steps/day and have my name randomly chosen. I won!

Besides winning and the health benefits of walking more, using a Fitbit gave me illustrations of truth applicable to our spiritual health. First, my Fitbit is specific to me. When I activated it, I entered my height, weight, gender, and which wrist I would wear it on. To apply this spiritually, our relationship with God is personal and specific. From Matthew 10:30, God knows how many hairs are on your head.

If you have many hairs, your head is an image of God's intimate attention. If you have more bare than hair, take this promise to the bank: in Matthew 6:8, it says God knows what we need before we ask Him. God knows everything, even the pain coming our way.

Another truth illustrated: every morning, my Fitbit's count of steps is back at zero. I start again, walking to rack up the steps. Likewise, we do our spiritual walk daily. We need to be consistent. When we persevere, God can count on us and use us as His co-laborers. Let me elaborate on this point even when tragedies like mass shootings strike our hearts, we need to stand firm for love and unity. Off and on for the past week, MercyMe's song "Even If" has been playing in my head: "I know You're able and I know You can/ Save through the fire with Your mighty hand/But even if You don't/ My hope is You alone... You've been faithful/You've been good."[12] I believe God wants these truths to strengthen us. Even when we are hurt, confused, and questioning, He is still faithful, good, and calling us to trust Him.

We all wonder why God allows evil events. Man has free will. Evil influences us. My faith reminds me we are in a spiritual war; God suffers alongside us when we make the wrong choices or suffer the wrong choices of others; our safety is in Him. How are we going to respond to tragedies? The enemy comes to kill and destroy, using fear and the tactic of divide and conquer. God's answer is the cross. He fought the battle with love. The power that won was God's. What looked like defeat was victory-in-the-making.

Today is our opportunity to love, operate in God's power, and walk in victory.

November 2017

Shaking is Coming

Days before, I had texted my friend my experience and questions. She and I are both busy people, so we had to make an appointment to talk. At the appointed time, I called. She didn't answer. She had warned me she might be busy with her grandbaby. It was still the beginning of my fifteen-minute work break, so I waited for her return call. Just two minutes before going back to my desk, I was thrilled to hear my phone ring. As a pastor and a gracious person with many friends, she has contact with multiple persons of faith. She hears what's going on. She and I have been friends for decades. I trust her relationship with God. I wondered what she was going to tell me.

The short time we had was long enough for my friend to confirm my experience, encourage me, and give me something to think over. Before giving you what my friend said, let me share one other piece of information. For a year, it seems like God's been whispering in my spirit, "Shaking is coming." We see shaking in our world. The political scene is in upheaval, our cultural ways are shifting, and even the ground is shaking. When we see the natural as a signpost for the spiritual, then we consider whether the unseen is also shaking.

My recent experience happened during times of prayer and quiet. There were two instances but connected, so I see them as one. At church, I felt a whirlwind on top of my head. It air-lifted something out of me. I now feel freer. That night, as I was lying quietly before falling asleep, the outer shell that is my body was a whirlwind. I get dizzy on a swing set, but this didn't make me dizzy because it wasn't my insides spinning. Only my outsides. This whirlwind experience was unexpected and puzzling but not scary. I had a sense of God's peace. I trusted God.

My friend said she's been traveling lately and hearing stories similar to mine from many people. The faith community's understanding is about God's present-day actions. Just as He has been intimating that a shaking is coming, the shaking is now here. It's accompanied by a whirlwind that lifts off us what we do not need to be carrying. My friend experienced a long-forgotten issue released from her grasp.

Hebrews 12:27–28 says God will shake created things and that His kingdom that cannot be shaken will remain. It's a call to worship Him and hang on to Him because He is eternal. With Him, there is joy. That's the good news.

November 2017

Shaking is Here

It's happening, and it's exciting. In November 2017, I shared:

For a year, it seems like God's been whispering in my spirit, "Shaking is coming." We see shaking in our world. The political scene is in upheaval, our cultural ways are shifting, and even the ground is shaking. When we see the natural as a signpost for the spiritual, then we consider whether the unseen is also shaking.

My understanding of what's coming is based on Hebrews 12:27–28, which says God will shake created things and that His kingdom that cannot be shaken will remain. It's a call to worship Him and hang on to Him because He is eternal.

Now, in January 2020, the shaking is manifesting as a shift, a call to turn abruptly, leave the old ways behind, think new thoughts, and prepare for what God is going to do next. I will illustrate. Recently reading Ephesians 1, I noticed that in the past, I had highlighted the blessings we receive. We are chosen to belong to God, holy and forgiven, through Jesus Christ. That is our confidence and joy. What my recent reading told me: God gives, chooses, decides, wants, and is grace. I experienced a sharpened awareness of what the verses say about God.

No longer was I looking at what I receive from Jesus. Instead, what stood out to me was who God is. I didn't decide to refocus. The change of focus was done for me. Do you notice the difference?

I believe we are all being called first to know who we are in Christ and then focus on God. It's all about who God is. He is not only the center of it all. He is it. This is a call for total surrender to our commander-in-chief. Not me and you and our plans. This is preparation for God's anointing to fall upon us in greater measure for His end time victories. He is going to need vessels to use for His outpouring of healings, deliverances, and salvations.

Do you want to be used by God for mighty exploits? Using the image of still waters being stirred and that stirring signaling God's readiness to act, I am telling you the waters are stirring! Jump in!

Focusing on God in my reading of the Bible has grown my awareness of who He is and what He values. For example, after reading John 3:16, one could say God loves us so much, He gave up His Son to die for us, and now we can go to heaven. That is good news! We can also receive from that verse that God loves, God gives, and God saves. When I shift my focus from myself to God, I experience a fresh closeness with Him. It's the difference between seeking the gifts or the Gift-giver.

Remember Hebrews 12:26–28. It's time to press in and hang on to the one who is eternal. May God the Father give you knowledge and wisdom. May you know who you are in Christ. And may Holy Spirit empower you! In Jesus' name. Amen.

January 2020

Comfort and Hope

Blessed [gratefully praised and adored] be the God and Father of our Lord Jesus Christ, the Father of mercies and the God of all comfort, who comforts *and* encourages us in every trouble so that we will be able to comfort *and* encourage those who are in any kind of trouble, with the comfort with which we ourselves are comforted by God.

2 Corinthians 1:3–4 (AMP)

...your faith and hope are [centered and rest] in God.

1 Peter 1:21 (AMP)

Your Life Has a Purpose

Your life has a purpose. You are not alone. Your life is inside God's control.

Are you angry or afraid? Are you questioning God's goodness, power, or even existence? I want to help. God is not doing this to you. Evil exists. Evil is like a roaring, fiercely hungry lion looking for someone to devour (1 Peter 5:8, NIV). But evil's existence is necessary because it allows us the freedom to make choices. At the same time, we know that from the beginning this freedom has created the opportunity for wrong choices (Genesis 3, NIV). Wrong choices can have life and death consequences, like driving the wrong way on a one-way street. To make matters worse, it's not always our choices that make us vulnerable to mishaps and disasters. Sometimes we suffer the consequences of someone else's wrong choices.

When we suffer, we may ask, "Why is God letting this happen to me?" We could answer ourselves, "Why not me?" Because no matter who suffers, it's always one of God's children. All of us are God's creations, loved by God. Remember: God has a plan for you personally, to give you hope and a future. If something tries to train wreck that plan, God can use that train wreck for His purposes. The cross, this side of the resurrection, looked like a train wreck.

As God's creation, we are like a pot made by a potter. Is it the pot's place to ask the potter why he made him as he did? Does anyone have the audacity to question the Supreme Almighty (Romans 9:20–21)? But this understanding is not to be experienced like Dorothy and her companions with the Wizard of Oz. God does not rule with thunder blasts, intent on His own authoritative stance. He is not a dictator.

God rules by love for the purpose of a loving relationship. We can't totally understand, but there are even purposes served by having enemies. God tolerates, for now, those who are against Him so He can show us His glory at work (Romans 9:22–23). In the midst of the battle, the sweetness of God compels, strengthens, heals us.

When we overcome evil, we have times of joyful triumph.

There's a purpose for your pain. That is the thesis of Ron Carpenter's book, *The Necessity of an Enemy: How the Battle You Face Is Your Best Opportunity.*[13] Also, Ephesians 6 (NIV) says God needed this battlefield of life to show His victory over evil.

What do you think about what I've shared? Get strength by losing yourself in your love for God. If you can't do that, ask God to give you love for Him. God is the source of our being and doing (Acts 17:28, NIV). Ask for His grace: His favor with you.

Miracles Still Happen Today

Do you believe in miracles? When someone emerges unharmed from a major car accident, we say it was a miracle they survived. We talk about the miracle of birth. My brother-in-law can tell you about the miracle of being healed. He went into the hospital with abdominal pain. The doctors did tests and discovered he had major liver problems and a spot on his pancreas. The doctor wanted him to have surgery right away because it looked like aggressive cancer had invaded the pancreas. The surgeon was more conservative than the doctor. He wanted to put a scope down my brother-in-law's throat so he could look at the pancreas up close.

My brother-in-law is a man of faith and asked for people's prayers. He had hundreds of people praying for him. The result? The next time the doctors examined him, his pancreas was spotless and, after eight months of treatment, his liver will be good for another thirty years. That's fine. He can live with that. Miracles are always good things, marvelous occurrences. They inspire hope. They encourage us. They serve life.

I want to tell you about another miracle that has encouraged me. You can find it recorded in Sonny and Julie Arguinzoni's book *Treasures Out of Darkness*. The short version is that Julie is married to Pastor Sonny. Their ministry is mainly to drug addicts, prostitutes, and gang members. In the early days of ministry, he was on the city streets, telling people about the hope and new life available to them. In the process of talking with them, he invited them home for dinner. Julie was usually agreeable to him bringing home unexpected guests, but it caused her some panic this time. In their early days, they were living below the poverty level. All they had in the cupboard was one and a half cups of pancake mix.

What Julie did next was rely on God. She reminded God that her husband was telling their guests that God was available to be their savior and provider. She knew if she said there was no food, that would make God look like a poor provider. She asked God for a miracle. She asked Him to do the same thing with the pancake mix as He did with the five loaves and two fishes that fed more than five thousand people.

God answered her prayer. Julie poured the pancake mix and the correct amount of water into a bowl and stirred. She prayed and stirred. Stirred and prayed. The cup and a half of the mix filled the bowl to the rim. Julie had to get a larger bowl. She kept stirring and praying, and the pancake mix reached the rim of that bowl. What started as maybe enough mix to feed three people fed ten, with pancakes left over![14] Are you familiar with the story of the five thousand fed with the five loaves and two fishes (John 6:1–14)? It was something Jesus did. He is available to do the same thing today!

These real-life stories encourage me. I believe in miracles. And just behind the miracles, I believe in the one who provides the miracles. I believe in God, who is available as a savior and provider. He is the giver of hope and encouragement. He is the source of life.

My friend Julie and her husband are now the leaders of a ministry that reaches around the world, Victory Outreach International. It is in twenty-four countries. God has continued to be their provider. My brother-in-law recently joined the rest of the family to celebrate a miracle: the marvelous occurrence of Jesus' resurrection. I hope you had a good Easter and that you have hope and are encouraged.

April 2007

Love Is Stronger than Death

Recently, a woman in my community died. I know some of her friends, and I've heard her husband preach. He is a friendly, God-loving man. His wife died suddenly, without warning. The way I heard it, she was seemingly fine, and then she stopped breathing.

I don't need to tell you about death. Death is crisis and tears. What I want is to offer you comfort. Yes, she died, but it was her physical self that died. Her spiritual self didn't die. That's what eternal life is all about.

The personal experience I can share with you about life after death has to do with my grandma. I was with her when she died. She was a generous Christian woman, and it was a blessing to be there with her. After she took her last breath, I stared at her face. I realized she was no longer there. It seemed to me that she was across the room from me. I asked her what it was like, and I heard inside myself, "Flowers and dancing." My first thought in response was, *But Grandma, you don't dance.* My next thought was, *Well, I guess she does now.*

I wonder how it was for Linda. I wonder a lot of things about her sudden departure, but I do not question her final destination. She claimed Jesus as Savior and Lord. She's with Him in glory. Hallelujah. Linda died, but she still lives. Therefore, she is still loving. If she loved someone while she was here, she would not stop loving them because she's not physically with them. When my husband goes out of the country on mission trips, does he stop loving me just because he's not at home with me? Love is stronger than separation. Love is stronger than death.

I have learned something about death in my time of grieving for Linda and praying for her family and friends. Please forgive me if this sounds trite: but death is a doorway, not a destination. It is not a location. It is something that happens. I am no longer going to use the euphemism *passing away.* My fear of death is less now.

I have also learned about love, and my suggestion to us all: when struggling, choose to love, and you will gain victory. You will gain the victory because love is stronger than death. I want to say it again. Death is not the last word because love is stronger than death.

Are you wondering about all this? I imagine someone reading this could have questions about why I can say all this as fact and not hedge my bets. I have shared my experience with my grandma. I have shared the understandings I have received through prayer that death is not the last word. Now I want to remind you of the one who is love. He conquered death.

By His life and death, Jesus showed His love for us. With His resurrection, He showed His power. If you want to read about Jesus' rising from the dead from an unbiased point of view, go to Matthew 28. There were guards on duty at the tomb, not Jesus' followers but the governor's men. Matthew 28:11 says the guards reported to the chief priests there was an earthquake, an angel rolled the stone away from the front of the tomb, and the tomb was empty. Jesus was no longer there. That's the power of love over death.

December 2007

God Covered the Cost

God gave me a gift for you. I was thinking about financial ups and downs, and I told God I wanted to encourage folks. He gave me a real-life example of His help being available. Here's what happened.

At the beginning of October, I bought a plane ticket to go to a women's leadership conference offered by my church. A week after I purchased my plane ticket, the deadline arrived to register for the conference, so I paid $100. A week after I registered, my plans changed, and I could no longer go. I was disappointed at not being able to go and see my friends and hear the conference speakers and go on an adventure and receive God's blessings. Who would not be disappointed? But a greater good was served by my staying home, so I did.

Because the conference registration was non-refundable, I had to figure out how to deal with the lost $100. After all, $100 is two months of water bills and a small bag of groceries. I made some phone calls. The woman in charge of receiving the conference registration told me I could transfer it. Someone else could use it, and I could get my money back from them. I learned of a friend who had not made the registration deadline. I called that friend. She thought she would have to pay the registration plus a late fee when she got to the conference. When I called her, she was thrilled to buy my registration. She didn't have to pay the additional charge for late registration, and she could have her registration before going to the conference. I was happy. I was going to get back my $100.

Then, God showed His hand. In the process of making phone calls, I had called my husband at work to let him know that we had a credit with Delta Airlines for my canceled plane trip. That was good. I didn't mention the registration money because that piece was still in progress.

Twenty minutes after I sold the registration to my friend, my husband Gilbert called, very excited. He said God took care of the registration. A Christian man at his work gave Gilbert $100. He said God told him to. Gilbert said he knew right away the $100 was to cover the registration. And I told him I would tell my friend she didn't need to pay me. Gilbert said, "What?" He didn't know anything about someone already buying the registration, but we were both blessed when I told him God had paid, so now my friend wouldn't have to pay, and this blessed her. God used me as a conduit for the transaction, and this blessed me. The man at Gilbert's work was blessed to confirm that he heard God right and that God used him to bless others. God took care of each of us.

I want to do more than encourage you with this story. I want to remind you Jesus cares about the details of your life: even about how much is or is not in your wallet. Look to him to take care of you. God be with you.

November 2008

Not Coincidence nor Luck

It is not possible for the following to have happened without God. It cannot be coincidence or luck because those two notions are without life, and the following is a matter of knowledge and life. If, after reading Scott Montgomery's account, you choose to disbelieve it, then the only way to discount what he's saying is to decide he's lying. Here's his story of what happened last January.

From Scott

My wife and I started off this new year with some very heavy financial burdens. We had to have an X amount of money by the 30th of January, and no foreseeable way of attaining that amount. We gave our problem to the Lord in prayer and faith that he would somehow help us. First off, about the middle of the month, I got a notice that a long outstanding and couldn't pay debt (sic) of about $25,000.00 had been canceled. Yes the notice said, debt canceled! Well, I still had to have that other X amount debt by January 30. On the twenty-sixth of the month, one of the pastors from our church called and asked me if I could help him move some furniture with him, and of course I said yes. I met him at the storage room, and when I got in his truck with him he was smiling and handed me an envelope and said manna from heaven Scott. I opened the letter up, and inside was a check from our church for the exact amount I had to have in four days. Well I broke down and started to cry, and it is not a pretty sight to see a 300 pound tattooed hippy biker, now saved by the blood of Jesus! Crying like a little kid!

But anyway, my pastor said that someone came to him and told him that the Lord had laid a burden on his heart to give this money to me. He didn't know my name but described me to him. No one, not even my wife, knew how much we had to have by the end of the month!! A total praise the Lord hallelujah blessing to a stranger from a stranger! The amount he gave was within pennies of the needed amount! We have an *awesome* God, and to Him I give all the honor, praise, and glory that He a *king* deserves![15]

Dear Reader, it's me again. I have had similar experiences. During a season when my husband and I needed additional finances, we received help from an unexpected source. An evangelist was visiting. Usually, the congregation seeks to bless the evangelist with finances, but when my husband shook his hand, the evangelist slipped him $20. We had made no mention of our need. It is easy for me to see God's hand at work as in Scott's situation.

If you need help, I recommend Psalm 91:14–15. It details what God calls us to do and what He promises. Allow me to paraphrase. God says that if you hold on to Him for dear life, He will get you out of any trouble. He will give you the best of care if you will only get to know and trust Him. Call, and God will answer and be at your side in bad times. He will rescue you.

There is no coincidence or luck. There is only God's grace.

January 2009

There Is Hope

How do you let go of something? You consciously loosen your grip on it until the thing either fades, falls, floats, or scampers away. Conversely, how do you hang on to something? If you are a young child and your mom wants you out of the car and into the dentist's office to have some cavities filled, you hold on to the car's door for all you're worth. Your mom has to pry your fingers one at a time off that door. All while you are screaming and crying, and passersby are wondering if they should call the authorities, and your mom is getting frustrated, you hang on.

Hanging on is something we do consciously. It takes strength and sometimes strategy. I want to talk about hanging on to hope. We know hope's power. In an experiment with rats in water, the rats swam for hours before most of them succumbed to drowning. Some survived because the experimenter rescued them. In a repeat of the experiment, the rats who were rescued once before swam longer. Hope helps us persevere.

I am going to argue with myself for a minute. Hang on. The story about the rats is good because it is factual, and there is a marked difference between their abilities to persevere. On the other hand, the second group of rats ended up drowning just like the first group. What good is that? Here's what we can learn from the second group of rats: hope empowers, but it matters a great deal where you place your hope. Can the object of your hope live up to your expectations?

The Apostle Paul endured many hardships, but he had hope to share with his protégé, Timothy. He told the younger man, "That is why I am suffering as I am. Yet I am not ashamed, because I know whom I have believed and am convinced that he is able to guard what I have entrusted to him for that day" (2 Timothy 1:12, NIV).

I have hope. God's Word is full of His promises to us. It has example after example of His power. It shows us His love for us. I have hope because I have experienced God's love. In the thirty-five plus years that I have been a Christian, I have known God's love surrounding me and heard His *I love you* in my spirit. I have hope because I have read biographies and autobiographies of faithful Christians who testified about God's awesome love toward them. I have hope because I serve not a god of the past who came and died but a God who came, died, and rose from the grave. He's alive again and alive still. Praise God.

In my briefcase, I carry a hope notebook. I have written down scriptures that are meaningful to me and instructions God's given me. I review these pages often. They help keep my flame of hope lit. You could do the same thing. Here is a good scripture to start with

> "For I know the plans I have for you," declares the Lord, "plans to prosper you and not to harm you, plans to give you hope and a future. Then you will call upon me and come and pray to me, and I will listen to you. You will seek me and find me when you seek me with all your heart. I will be found by you," declares the Lord.
>
> Jeremiah 29:11–14 (NIV)

That scripture comes from Jeremiah 29, and it can go wherever you go. You could cut it out of this newspaper and tuck it in your wallet. You could memorize it and let it encourage your heart. God loves you. Hang on to that for all you're worth.

March 2009

Hope Is Available

Some families are quiet, but I belong to a loud family: My church family, that is. In my church, we clap while we sing. During the preaching, we say, "Amen," and the preaching is enthusiastic. We are loud because we are so grateful. Our church is eighty percent former drug addicts, gang members, and prostitutes. Those were their former lives, but now they are new persons in Christ. We recently held a rally in the parking lot of our newest church location. The PA system amplified our music and message. At the rally, I heard several life stories from different people.

One woman told how she had been born to a mom and dad who were both heroin addicts. She and her siblings were taken from their family at an early age. When she was thirteen years old, her mom got her back only to exploit her and her sisters for drug money. Her mom died when she was fourteen, but by then, this woman was an addict herself. She is now safe, free, and giving God thanks for her new life. She is in a Victory Outreach recovery facility. One woman told how she used to beat her children to make them quiet so she could go in the bathroom and shoot up. Another woman told how she sold herself for $1 so she could have drug money.

The stories are heart-rending, but they all have the same ending. These women essentially said someone told me about God. I gave God a chance. Now, I'm thankful to Him. I didn't get a chance to say anything at the rally, but if I had, I would have shared three points:

You may wonder why we are out here spending a Saturday morning telling you our personal stories. You may think we are a bit too loud or bold, but we're passionate. You may wonder why we're here. Here's why: we know what it's like to be tired, worn out, and lost. If you're feeling any of that, we want to help you. We know what being lost is and we know where to find hope, joy, and love.

We want you to know there is *hope* to replace depression, *joy* to take the place of despair, and love for everyone, no matter who they are or what is going on. Hope is not a wish for something. *Hope* is not some vague knowledge that maybe everything will turn out all right. Hope is a living spark that ignites the dry wood in a person's heart and sets that heart aflame with possibilities and promises. When I was depressed, hope was like a window opening. It surprised me and awakened me. That hope is available in Jesus.

Finally, you can trust what we are telling you. Those women were beat up from the feet up, and now they live with hope and joy in God. We really do feel for you and want to share all this goodness with you. God really does love everyone. Sometimes people can be selective about who they care for and who they don't care for, but God loves everyone. No matter whether that person is black, brown, white, blue, purple, green, rich, poor, up, down, or sideways.

God is a good God, and He is faithful. He has been good to me for thirty-five years. I'm sure He is not going to stop now.

July 2009

Power of Love, Family, and God

Dillon is just eighteen years old as of last July. He has already seen more and been through more of life's crises than I went through in the first thirty years of my life. He's had close relatives die. He's seen drug use and violence up close. As his stepmom, I tell him he's rich in moms: his birth mom, the mom who raised him when he was little, and me.

I've known Dillon since he was four years old. That's when I met and married his dad. What I remember about Dillon's childhood is playing many games of hide and seek and trying to catch the neighbor's llama when it got loose. I remember teaching him his vowels and how to swim.

Last June, at the end of his high school career, Dillon wrote a poem that touched my heart. He wrote, from his heart, about his life. I have his permission to share it with you. It is a witness to the power of love, family, and God

I'm From…

I'm from being born to a daddy Who was hooked on heroin
And a mother I wouldn't meet 'til I was seventeen.

I'm from being a little baby rescued from foster care
And driven across this country

To be cared for by an aunt who would be my "mama."
I'm from growin' up in a "ghetto house."

Where breakfast was cheerios with water
Or ice cream from the carton.

I'm from being a tough, young boy who knew no rules
Surrounded by drugs and violence

And a crazy gangster life.
I'm from "blood is everything, man."

A big family, fun times, tragic times
A mama giving all she had to keep us together

I'm from losing—losing the people I loved the most
From feeling my world end when my mama died

And learning to hate goodbyes.
I'm from being given an amazing new life

With my "cleaned up" dad and his wife—My new stepmom.
I'm from learning about God and miracles,

New values, new hopes
And new dreams

I'm from beginning to like who I am
And showing the world who I can be

And believing in a future for me.
I'm from "family is everything,"

But so are my friends.
And in my heart, I still hate to say goodbyes.

September 2009

Do the Right Thing

As children, we are taught that if we do as we're told, we won't get in trouble. In other words, to avoid stress and pain, do the right thing. As we grow up, *doing the right thing* can become a way of trying to control life. Of course, we cannot control much, but we try. Additionally, *doing the right thing* is sometimes impossible because we do not all live by the same rules. We have diverse backgrounds, live with different paradigms, and disagree on absolutes. Thus, conflict occurs. I want you to do the right thing by behaving in a certain manner. You want me to do your right thing, and you get upset when I don't.

Who gets to decide what *the right thing* is? In families, at the workplace, and driving a car, the one with authority decides on *rightness*. Parents decide for their children, bosses for their employees, the government for drivers. But what about in war where each side says, "Believe my way or die."?

Last November, I heard about some Christian missionaries facing ISIS. We have all heard horrific accounts. These missionaries were afraid because ISIS was literally down the block, but they knew God had called them to be His voice and hands at that place at that time. They asked us to cover them with showers of prayer. One kept asking for help to know what to do and to do it.

What is one to do when faced with evil? French consul general Denis Barbet says they are "not afraid."[16] To that, I say, "Amen." *No fear* is a good rallying cry to encourage and unite those who otherwise might crouch alone in the dark. I'll say it again, "Yes. I agree." But in the moment of hearing footsteps at the door, we need more than a rallying cry. We need to know the one who is *no fear*. We need to know who is the ultimate authority. Hopefully, we know we are where He wants us to be. To know God has called upon us for such a time is encouraging.

What if one's mind goes blank while one's heart is screaming for any way out at all? Grown men have been known to soil their pants at such times. Call out "Jesus!" There's power in His name. If I had been the one that missionary asked for help, I would have told him the same thing the person he was talking to did. I would have assured him of people praying for him. I would have reminded him demons tremble in fear in Jesus' presence. They know who has the authority, and it is not them.

With only moments left, remember those who have gone before and look to your future. When others faced death for Christ's sake, He was there with them. Stephen saw him standing beside the Father in heaven. The three in the fire were joined by a fourth and were delivered. When Christ faced death, He conquered it so we wouldn't have to fear it. Hold on to heaven, where there is no pain or darkness, only full, abundant, never-ending love. We will walk on streets of gold and live forever in that love.

February 2015

God Answers with His Presence

On the trapeze without a safety net, I am submitting this column for publication without my mom's critique. She has been my personal editor, but now she is in the glory of heaven. I'm an orphan, left to recall as best as possible her advice: be clear, be open, don't preach.

God is faithful. My mom, Mrs. Janssen, went to heaven at age eighty-one. She was at home. That was an answer to her prayers. I assume she also petitioned God to take care of her children. He's been faithful to answer that prayer too. I've been on a personal journey of grief for ten months. I am not asking for sympathy or condolences. My purpose is to share with you God's goodness. He has not left my side.

In the beginning, I woke up every morning to the jab, "Mom's dead. Mom died." I asked myself, "How could that be? She's always been." I wondered how long it would take before I believed it. It seemed as if I was in a canyon. A big empty space defined only by steep walls, making an exit impossible. I felt trapped and hurt, and I couldn't do anything about it. I tried to get out of the canyon. My heart was no help. Sorrow hit me with a thud, and my eyes dripped tears. My mind wrestled with the question, "What is death?" I couldn't grasp it. Death is an event. My mom walked through the door that opened for her. It slammed in my face. I called on my faith, reminding myself that she is in heaven. I was glad for her and sad for me.

I went to sleep at night clutching a little stuffed doggie: my mom's hospital and bedtime companion. When I was holding him, I felt closer to her. I would visit my hurt and cry myself to sleep. After two months of this, enough! God said, "Stop clutching your misery to yourself." Even though I questioned the correctness of my ever feeling better, God was right. I was habitually wallowing in my pain. I put her doggie away.

My experience is of God's shepherding care. Not only does He provide guardrails, but He comforts me. Something caught me the other day, reminding me mom is no longer available for my phone calls. I understood God to say, "Yes. She's no longer with you. I am your parent." God watches over us. He answered my need the moment I had it. He understood my feeling of abandonment. He answered with His presence.

We know we will see them again. We will see our loved ones who have died in Jesus' arms. My mom and I are going to dance together when I get to heaven. She's gone, but she still lives. I miss her, but I'm not overwhelmed anymore. I can't be with my mom now because God's plans and purposes for me have not yet been fulfilled. He holds the order of our days in His hands. And in those instances, when I want something to soothe the ache, I say, "Praise you, Jesus." He is my resting place.

June 2017

Maturation

And we all, with unveiled face, *continually* seeing as in a mirror the glory of the Lord, are *progressively* being transformed into His image from [one degree of] glory to [even more] glory, which comes from the Lord, [who is] the Spirit.

2 Corinthians 3:18 (AMP)

Holy Spirit Questions

I have adapted the following from a class I taught.

Holy Spirit used to ask me, as I was quiet at the end of a day, "How often did you remember Jesus today?" It was a convicting question because I'd not given much thought to Jesus. I'd been too busy with myself. I didn't feel like Holy Spirit was rebuking me but encouraging me to do my day differently and get closer to Jesus.

Because of the Holy Spirit's question, I considered how I could think about Jesus more often. I decided I could say *hallelujah* when something good happened. Now, after doing that for years, I am known for being a *hallelujah* lady. Another idea was to wear a cross on my hand to see it, rather than on a necklace. God gave me a beaded bracelet design that places a cross in the middle of the back of my hand. Now I've made and given away many bracelets. They are fun to make and have become a ministry to others.

One other thing that has helped me see Jesus in my daily life is by becoming a newspaper columnist. I have a column titled "Faithfully" in the *Woodburn Independent*. My goal in writing the column is to show people God exists and He loves us. I write true stories of God's presence in my life and in the lives of others. I write about the encouragement He gives and the miracles He does. As I record and share with others, I witness to myself.

If you want to remember Jesus more often in your day, I recommend to you:

1. Praise God throughout the day. Make it a habit to thank Him.

2. Place visual reminders of Him in your environment.

3. Tell people, including yourself, about the goodness of God.

While I was writing a column one day, the Holy Spirit dropped another question on me, "What would you be like if you believed that Jesus lived inside you?" Do understand that when Holy Spirit asked me this, I'd already been a Christian for decades. He wasn't referring to me accepting Jesus as my savior. He was asking me to live as an empowered Christian, one who knows that I have everything I need for a successful, victorious life. I have everything that Jesus Christ has: life, power, and authority. Every time the Bible says that I have something "in Christ," it means I have it today.

I understand the Holy Spirit to be saying it is time we use what we have. Compare it to what Jesus said to Paul after He knocked him off his horse. As recorded in Acts 26:16 (NIV), "Now get up and stand on your feet. I have appeared to you to appoint you as a servant and as a witness of what you have seen of me and what I will show you."

Let's get up. When I start my day asking Jesus, "What do you want to do today?" then I notice I am more involved with people. I am not as self-contained and am more accepting of others. I feel calmer because I don't have to be in control.

This is a proactive way to live. It reminds me of Bill Johnson's teaching that Roku served me the other night. I started the evening watching segments of Jonathan Cahn. After they were over, Pastor Johnson, author and Christian life speaker, came on. He was speaking to a full auditorium. It was 2012 at a NY/LA Conference. Pastor Johnson's subject was the power of Christ evident in our lives. He said we need to live in response to God instead of in defense against the devil. We should not let the enemy dictate our agenda. That's not his right.[17]

It's time to laser in on Jesus, get up, and enjoy the adventure that awaits us. I'm thankful for the Holy Spirit's nudging questions and the riches we have in Christ.

How Does One Die?

How does a person say *yes* to death? The desire to live, some call it the survival instinct, is well documented. Even the untrained will behave in ways that support the continuance of their life. Babies suckle for nourishment and cry when they need attention. Grown men act heroically in order to survive. We heard about the man who was hiking solo in a lonely canyon. When he got trapped, pinned inside a crevice, he cut his arm off in order to free himself.[18] With this man who acted courageously I will include the man who, for twelve years, got away with attempted murder but then turned himself in to the police. Proverbs 28:17 (NIV) states, "A man tormented by the guilt of murder will be a fugitive 'til death." I imagine even attempted murder has enough guilt with it that a person would live with ears sensitive to every police siren and knock on the door.

Just like the physically trapped man, the weight of his past trapped this man. He had to sacrifice his freedom to attain his life fully. He said he turned himself in because he found religion and wanted to take responsibility for his actions. I believe him. When a person comes into a relationship with the living God, this is often a call for heroics. It's a good thing God provides us the power to do what He wants to be done.

For me, I understand God to be asking for my total commitment. More than thirty years ago, I heard Jesus in my spirit ask me if I was willing to die for him. I said I was. I never asked, "Do you mean die to my flesh or be martyred?" Ten years later, He gave me Galatians 2:20 (NIV), which says I have been crucified with Christ and now I live by faith in Jesus. This answered my fear of eventual martyrdom to some degree.

I believe God is real, and He gives me abundant living. The horizon is broader than I can imagine. Therefore, I am willing to consider a life of dying. How does one prepare to die? Ecclesiastes 7:2 (NIV) says, "Death is the destiny of every man; the living should

WHAT DOES A CHRISTIAN LOOK LIKE?

take this to heart." I like what I heard in Petra's worship song about a "love stronger than death."[19] Jesus faced death because of His love for us. He didn't back down. He loved His father and was obedient. He loved us and went all the way through death to victory. Hallelujah. It seems the best way to die is the same as the best way to live: in love.

On my dad's deathbed, he accepted Jesus as his savior. He finally accepted Jesus' offer of love. Half an hour later the angels escorted him to heaven. That was a good dying. My niece had juvenile diabetes and after years of hospital stays, her body gave up. In the last conversation I had with her, she knew her time was coming. She told me the provisions she had made for her dad and stepmom to take care of her young daughter. She talked about other family members and she said she was going to give herself to God for His use. Her focus was on loving family and God. I was with my sister-in-law Michelle for the couple of days before she passed into Jesus' arms. I was there beside her bed when she startled me by declaring, "Suzanne!" I said, "What?" "I love you," she said.

My family has taught me love is the most important thing. In my life with my husband Gilbert, he has told me thousands of times he loves me. His love has overcome my childhood observation that husbands don't love wives. Somehow, Gilbert's love helps me receive God's love. I can't explain how that happens, but here are two more thoughts on dying. Living in submission to God's will prepares us to submit when it's our time to leave for heaven. That's God's care for us and efficiency. He accomplishes two things: leading us into a fuller life and preparing us for our last day. Also, God gives us grace for getting saved, grace for living, and grace for dying. My advice to myself and you: Love God, love others, ask God for grace.

June 2007

Jesus Is Coming Back

If someone told you the world was ending soon, how would you feel? Would you feel excited or scared? At first, I was scared and confused, but then I understood what was going on. Here's what happened. I enjoy teaching. I especially enjoy teaching adults about God and spiritual topics. Several Sundays ago, it was my turn to teach the little kids' Sunday school class. It's only my turn once a month. It's not a burden, but I was nervous because I did not know the children well, and I was not sure I could keep their attention and teach them something. Five-year-olds are fun, but they are a very different class from teaching thirty-five-year-olds.

I was nervous that morning, and in my prayer time, I asked God to help me. What I understood God to tell me was, "Jesus came (back then). Jesus is coming again." This was wonderful to hear because it changed my focus. I was no longer nervous about teaching the little kids. I was excited with the reminder that what we see here is not all we get: God's real, Jesus is real, and there's more to come! That Sunday morning went well.

A couple of mornings later, I was reading my Bible, and a verse jumped off the page at me, "He shall live again and God's program shall prosper in his hands" (Isaiah 53:10, LB). This verse is about Jesus. Even though He was crucified, He will be alive and see the glorious outcome of His sacrifice. Very soon after reading the above verse from Isaiah, my sister-in-law called. In the course of the conversation, she told me that she had an encounter with the Holy Spirit in church. She understood Him to say something like, "Hold tight, for one day He is coming back for His people."

These instances are all encouraging, especially taken just one at a time. I got scared and confused when they started to come at me from several directions. I got scared because this is big news, and I wasn't sure what to make of it. Was God telling me to stand on the street corner and tell everyone? How soon was Jesus coming? Was I supposed to quit my job? I got confused because I believe everything the Bible says is true. Matthew 24:36 (NIV) says, "No one knows about that day or hour, not even the angels, nor the Son, but only the Father." God the Father is the only one who knows when Jesus is coming back. No one will know the time until it actually happens. There seemed to be a contradiction between what I understood from God and what Scripture says.

What I did next dispelled my fear and cleared up my confusion: I took some time out. I went away to a quiet place and pleaded with God to tell me why He told me about Jesus' return. What I understood at that point was that God wants me to have joy. God wasn't asking me to take any action. He was offering me a joyful perspective on life. I was not given dates or a time. I was reminded of a reality. We just celebrated Jesus' birth, and a long time ago, that really happened. I'm not sure when, but Jesus is really coming back again. That is a reason to have joy.

January 2008

Peace

I could feel the peace. To my eyes, what I saw was a small church in Astoria, Oregon. There was no service in progress. I was just a tourist looking around. And in my heart, peace. I was surprised at feeling that peace. I had not gone looking for it, but it was certainly there. I met someone connected with the church, and after she told me the church was one hundred years old, I understood. For one hundred years, people have been praying inside those walls in that place. Their prayers have gone up, and God's peace has come down.

I find the same peace at the Abbey in Mt. Angel. The sanctuary there is beautiful, physically and spiritually. I go there when I need that extra support. When my prayers seem jumbled or when I can't find any words, going to a place of prayer helps me.

I find the same peace by reading the Psalms. In fact, it was while reading a psalm that I re-lived the memory of the Astoria church. The writer David says,

> One thing I ask of the Lord, this is what I seek: that I may dwell in the house of the Lord all the days of my life, to gaze upon the beauty of the Lord and to seek him in his temple.

Psalm 27:4 (NIV)

What I experienced in that Astoria church, what I find at the Abbey, and what the Psalms give me is the assurance of God's closeness, the reminder of His goodness, a glimpse of Him. I think that is what David longed for: to be that close to His sustenance and peace.

Let's take this one step further. I am startled that we can be close to God. Whenever I think, *My body is a temple where God resides*, my next thought is, *Really*? I know it's true. I did ask God to come into my heart, but I am just me. I am a small human. I am definitely not perfect in anything. We're talking about the one who is all everything, all love, all power, and all glory, inside a five-foot six inch, fifty-two-year-old woman. It blows my mind. As my teenage son would say,

"That's crazy." In other words, it's a slippery thought. I cannot keep hold of it.

Maybe that's how it is with the grand things of God. They are too grand to sit still for us. They are not available for analysis. I know God loves us more than we can imagine. Psalm 103:11 (NIV) says, "For as high as the heavens are above the earth, so great is his faithful love for those who fear him." Note that here, *fear* means *respect*. Now that's beyond human figuring: His love for us is higher than heaven's distance from earth.

How are you doing with these ideas? Look at what happens when you tell yourself, "I am a temple for the living God." If this truth seems slippery or startling or surreal, don't force the issue. Maybe you are like me. Years ago, I gave myself to God, and I'm in love with Jesus. Still, it is a process for me to accept that the God of all creation and time is not far off somewhere. He is within me.

Even now, I chuckle and wonder at the thought, but what will my life be like when I can fully accept that truth? When we can walk in the confidence that God is inside, how will that change us? Will we walk more humbly? With more power? I recall a verse from Matthew 5:9 (NIV) which says, "Blessed are the peacemakers, for they will be called sons of God." Maybe we will be the reservoirs of peace for those persons seeking peace.

March 2008

Position of Forgiving Others

Thank goodness Police Chief Scott Russell is recovering. The chief and his family thank God for every victory gained and step made toward going home from the hospital and returning to our city's police department. Regarding the bomb, which killed two officers and seriously wounded Chief Russell, Mayor Kathy Figley said it was the darkest hour in the city of Woodburn's history. Were you in town that evening?

My husband had just picked me up from work. We drove toward that Mexican restaurant near Grocery Outlet, when we saw three police cars racing west on Mt. Hood, sirens loud. They were going fast. I knew something big had happened. I prayed. A lot of us prayed and continue to pray. We ask God to comfort the families of the slain heroes. We ask God to encourage Chief Russell and his family. We ask God to give us Himself in the midst of our anger, fear, and grief.

When God gives us Himself, we receive awareness of His goodness and His ways. God's way is He forgives. We wrong Him. He forgives us. I have always wondered about that part in the Lord's Prayer, which says, "Forgive us our sins just as we have forgiven those who have sinned against us" (Matthew 6:12, LB). When Jesus taught His disciples the prayer, He told them, God the Father will forgive us if we forgive others.

I ask you, how are we supposed to forgive the persons who placed that bomb in the bank? Because I was having a hard time even thinking about forgiving them, I spoke with Pastor Luis Molina of the Woodburn Foursquare Church. He loves God and loves Woodburn.

In part, Pastor Luis explained that when God tells us to forgive:

1. He is speaking to His children.
2. The ability to forgive comes after we have experienced God's forgiveness for us.

3. His forgiveness is based on His love, which opens the doors to a personal relationship with Him.

4. This relationship with Him teaches us to love and forgive.

I want to highlight that last point. In my conversation with Pastor, I wrestled with the idea of forgiving those who hurt my friends. Why would God tell me to do something so hard? How am I supposed to do it? Pastor Luis bottom-lined it, "Forgiveness is more than just a work of. Instead, it is a *position* God allows me to be in and it is very important to know that I have received it because of Jesus Christ."

It's like what Sister Okoye taught a new Christian in Mark Olsen's suspense thriller, *The Watchers*. The new Christian, Dylan, says, "I'm surprised and fairly confused... all this time and you haven't yet talked about do's and don'ts or getting clobbered for this or that sin."[20] Okoye tells him, "Well, don't get your hopes too high because following His commands for righteous living is definitely important."[21] And dear Reader, look what Okoye says next. She echoes Pastor Luis with, "The problem is most people get it backward. Living right is not the way you become saved by Him. It's the proof, the evidence, that you are in Him."[22] Obedience is a byproduct.

Pastor Luis wants us to know, "When I choose to forgive, I am in partnership with God so He can give me the grace to let go of the harm the other person has created. But also, I need His Holy Spirit to keep me in the path of forgiveness until I experience full freedom and restoration."

I do not yet have the freedom that comes with forgiving the bombers, but I have been liberated. I now realize forgiveness is not a work I have to do. Rather, it's a choice I make because of a relationship I have. I live and move and have my being in Jesus, my Savior. In step with Him, holding His hand day by day, life is easier. Hallelujah.

February 2009

God Is Not Just Mine

Two things I'll say upfront. I don't put bumper stickers on my car, and God is not just mine. Lots of people know Him. Since I began this monthly column, I've heard from some readers. One woman emailed me to say thanks for putting out a positive word about Christianity. One mom emailed greetings from her grown children. I used to work with them at a local restaurant fifteen years ago. They encouraged me to keep writing. What this tells me is that you and I are not alone. Of course, we know we're never alone. Jesus promised never to leave us. In addition to the wonderfulness of Jesus never leaving you, I want to assure you there are believers around you.

A customer came up to me at work recently. He almost blew me away. He thanked me for writing my column and said it was great. He said that, and then he was gone, but he packed so much enthusiasm into those two sentences! I say all this to make the point that I've seen that man before, but I didn't know he was a Christian. You probably have people around you who believe in Jesus, and you don't know it. Not all Christians wear religious jewelry, have gospel bumper stickers, and look for each conversation to include something exciting about God's goodness. I do two of the three, but my point is you can't tell a person believes in Jesus just by looking at them.

Therefore, I want to give you a gentle kick in the pants. Do you want to increase your joy? The easiest way to have more joy is to offer God to someone. When you hear someone sneeze, say, "God bless you." When I say it to people, they always appreciate it. Personally, I feel lonely when I am around other people in a market or wherever and sneeze, and no one says "Bless you." Also, when someone shares their troubles with you and your shoulder is getting wet with their tears, ask them if you could pray for them. I've never had anyone turn down prayer. If it's not possible to pray right then with them, I pray later by myself. One more opportunity to increase your joy is when something goes right. When you hear good news, try saying, "God is good!" or something similar.

Maybe this sounds like too much for you. For some, faith is a private issue. Some fear rejection if they put their beliefs out there for others to see. I hope you can look at it this way: your friend tells you she is thirsty. You offer her what you have in your refrigerator, some cold grape juice. She says, '"No, thank you." She's not rejecting you. She just doesn't want any grape juice right then.

I think it'll encourage you to hear from my mom. Here's what she said, upon proofing this column for me, "Just recently I was talking to a young lady, one of my physical therapists. She was telling me a little about her life. Something was missing in the conversation. I couldn't put my finger on it until I heard myself asking her, 'Did you ever ask God to help you with your life's plan?' She didn't answer, but she didn't run away either." My mom concludes with this comment, "I always say, 'God bless you for all day and night' when somebody around me sneezes. Everyone so far has said, 'Thank you.'"

There you have it, dear readers. In the beginning, I was afraid to speak up, but now it's fun. It's fun, and I'm always glad because I appreciate being able to express myself instead of stifling myself. Also, it's a joy when I speak up, and someone gets blessed. Finally, when I speak up, I am more available for God's use. With God, everything is an adventure!

November 2009

Being a Cheerful Giver

I wanted to do it anonymously, but now I'm going to put it in the newspaper. Just know that I didn't do it to get your applause. On a recent trip to California, my husband and I stopped for breakfast in a family-style restaurant. We had a good meal and were getting ready to go when I spotted a couple of men dressed in army fatigues. I had noticed them earlier walking toward the restaurant from their army vehicle, and now I saw them eating breakfast. I felt the impulse to pay for their breakfast. I went to the cashier and emptied all the coins from my purse, about $7 worth, and asked her if she'd put it toward their bill and tell them, "God bless you." She promised she would. I did it because I wanted to thank them for their service and support them in what they do. I did it anonymously because they don't need to know who I am. This way, the support can be from all of us.

I felt good about what I did. As we continued our travels, I thought about the two men being surprised by the gesture, and I hope they felt encouraged. I hope it made their day. I even hope it helps them keep going. They make sacrifices, and I reap the benefits. I am grateful to them. The amount I gave wasn't big, but that's not the point. The point is I wanted to give something to them. I didn't have to give it. I felt good about giving it.

Some scriptures teach us to give God some of our earnings and to do it cheerfully. You can imagine that sometimes it's hard to give up some of my finances. Money being so useful and, sometimes, in short supply, after all. I have put money into the offering plate for years. I've done it out of obedience. Over time, it has gotten easier to give to God because I've learned that a person cannot outgive God. Go ahead and try it. Give God something. He'll give you back more than you gave Him. That's just the way He is.

If money is not flowing out of your pocketbook just this moment, there are things you could give Him instead. Give Him a smile. Give Him a "Thank you." Tell Him He's awesome. Give Him an hour of consciously doing good for someone else. I'm not talking about karma. I'm talking about purposely doing something for God. What I believe will happen is that you'll find God smiling back at you.

Back to my story: Over the years, it has become easier to give to God. But now, it's even easier because I understand about being a cheerful giver. I was a cheerful giver when I gave toward the servicemen's breakfast. It was a pleasure to be able to show them my support. As I considered that cheerful giving, the insight that popped into my mind was that I could give to God in the same way. I have a lot to be thankful for. My thankfulness can serve me when I give Him my money. All I have to do is give with the mindset of being grateful for what He's done for me. This may seem like a small epiphany, but it's going to make my life a lot easier!

February 2010

God Knows You Love Him

When I love someone, there are three ways it could be. I could love them and:

1. They'd never know.
2. They'd know but not love me in return; or
3. They'd love me back.

Of these three, number three is preferable. Sometimes when my husband and I are saying, "I love you" to each other, one of us will say, "I'm glad you love me because I'd hate to be in love alone." To be in love alone is to be lonely. To love and be loved is a relationship and belonging.

The other day I had an experience in love that was short in length of time but high in impact. I was at church, enjoying the time set aside to worship God. What I heard in my spirit was, "I know that you love me." I understood it as God's gentle, loving voice. There was no one around speaking to me, and I didn't hear it with my ears. It wasn't something I told myself. I was so thrilled, I told one of my church friends, "God knows I love Him!" My friend didn't respond with the same level of excitement I was feeling so I think I didn't adequately share what had happened.

Of course, it's the truth. Since God knows all, He knows my feelings for Him. Also, if you would have asked me, "Do you think God knows you love Him?" I would have said, "I'm sure He does. I've told Him plenty of times." But, my friend, I'm not talking about knowing facts. I'm talking about experiencing love. When God spoke into me, I sensed His presence, and we had a moment of togetherness. Most of all, that moment was loving.

I wonder if these words in a book can tell you how God loves you. I'm not special. I'm just like you. I have goals, fears, a family to care for, and my weight to watch. Because you and I are the same under

God, you can own my experience for yourself. You can claim for yourself that God knows you love Him. God sees you. He recognizes you. You are known. He feels your love for Him. He values your love. He values being in a relationship with you. He loves you more than you can imagine.

I invite you to hold close to your heart this treasure of you and God, loving each other. When I think about Jesus loving people, I remember the story in Luke 10 (NIV) about Jesus, Mary and Martha. Jesus was at their home, and the two sisters were responding to Jesus' presence in two different ways. Martha was busy taking care of preparations and details. I imagine myself in Martha's position. She had invited Jesus over. He was there. She probably wanted the living room to be clean and something pleasing for her guest to eat. There was so much to do, but when she looked up from her "to do" list, she saw her sister Mary just sitting there. Mary was sitting with Jesus, listening to him. I imagine it was an intimate time, but Martha didn't see it that way. She complained to Jesus about Mary not helping her. What Jesus said to Martha shows us what He values.

He said, "Mary has chosen what is better" (Luke 10:42, NIV)! God doesn't need us to get our lives cleaned up and straightened before we come to Him. He wants us to come as we are and be with Him. He values spending time with you. He wants to be close to you.

He loves you. He knows you love Him. And He wants to sit with you in that love.

October 2010

Miraculous Living

What if I woke up in the morning and lived moment to moment in the holy? What would it look like? I imagine myself having no reluctance to leave brother blanket and sister pillow and sing praises to God. Imagine being joyful, being in the flow. Currently, I am in the habit of giving God thanks before my feet touch the floor. While waking up and still horizontal, I thank God for ten things. My list of ten changes from morning to morning but usually includes gratitude for my salvation. Being thankful puts me in a good mood. What would I need in order to live in that place of gratitude? I know some things I need to jettison. If I were free of anger and the desire to promote myself, I would be more available for joy. That's what I think. Is there any support for such theorizing?

God has made several promises to those who give up worry and striving. One of those promises encourages us to rejoice, relax, recall God is near, and reject anxiety. Instead, tell God what we need and receive His peace. Read the following

> Rejoice in the Lord always. I will say it again: Rejoice! Let your gentleness be evident to all. The Lord is near. Do not be anxious about anything, but in every situation, by prayer and petition, with thanksgiving, present your requests to God. And the peace of God, which transcends all understanding, will guard your hearts and minds in Christ Jesus.
>
> Philippians 4:4–7 (NIV)

If I lived my day as a totally happy camper, that would be good for me, but I want more. I want to have the goods and be able to share them with those who need them. If someone has a hurt finger, hurting heart, or something even more serious, I want God to use me to heal them and set them free. I want to be in such close synchronization with God that living in the miraculous becomes an everyday event. I am not looking for the divine to become ordinary, but the norm. I am not presenting an ideal that miracles become so common that they cease to be regarded as supernatural. I urge us to take Jesus seriously when He told the church we'd be doing greater things than He did.

What is getting in our way? Is it a lack of imagination? Our fear? Our lethargy? What is holding us back from living in the miraculous? Here's the most important question: can we break free from whatever is holding us back? I imagine something with long arms wrapped around us, restraining us. Not a pretty picture. Can we gain our freedom? Do you have the courage of a warrior? Can you focus on what you need to do and carry through with doing it? Can you do this even if it means turning off the television and forgoing that dessert, drink, or drug?

I am suggesting fasting because it builds discipline. With discipline, we can more easily follow God's instructions and marching orders. I am not claiming to be good at fasting. As far as I'm concerned, chocolate is one of the basic food groups. I am saying that I've benefited when I've stood firm and sought solace and satisfaction in God rather than sugar. God has even promised that when we do what He asks us to do, we'll have joy. See Psalms 119:35 (NIV), "Direct me in the path of your commands, for there I find delight." Joy is how we started this conversation. Let's count our blessings, receive God's joy, and enter the battle to attain miraculous living. How about it?

June 2011

God Is Center of Life

My pastor, Max Garza, says that in heaven, God speaks Spanish. Maybe it's true. I understand God's recent whispers to me as, "Cristo nacio. Cristo murio. Cristo vive." Translation: "Christ was born. Christ died. Christ lives." I'm not sure why He is telling me in Spanish, but I understand why He is telling me: the Christmas season includes the whole of Jesus' life and mission. Whether or not we include it in our Christmas messages, Jesus was born so one day He could die for us and be resurrected in victory. That mercy and power was accomplished. To all the above, I say, "Hallelujah!" The church has a reason for overwhelming joy.

The world can't provide joy. Only temporary escapes from pain. Someone has labeled these escapes "Wine, women, and song." They temporarily numb but are powerless to sustain and invigorate our lives. The church has a reason for joy unspeakable and full of glory. Even though the church is called to rejoice, sometimes we forget. We fall into thinking life revolves around us. You, personally. Me, personally. I want God to approve my plans/goals. Then, how do I behave when I don't get what I want? Do I feel sorry for myself and try to manipulate? Is that what we do?

When author and theologian Elton Trueblood looked at the church, he saw us being concerned with only ourselves. It's true. We are not perfect. He called for the church to be loving and not self-seeking because the world needs our testimony of good. Keep trying to be like Christ. Maintain your confidence in the gospel message. When those who are watching you see your continuing attempts and confidence, they will have hope. Therefore, how can we behave better? We can make ourselves available to Holy Spirit so He can work on us. When we listen and obey His promptings, He will lead us into being more like Christ.

All of history's Christians have had Holy Spirit, but today, His involvement in our lives is more prolific. Within churches, groups of men and women are dedicating themselves more completely to God. In addition to churches, groups of laypersons follow the Holy Spirit's leading. Full Gospel Business Men's Fellowship International is one such group. Christian television broadcasting is around the globe twenty-four hours a day, seven days a week. The Pentecostal and charismatic movements have been born. People are dreaming of Jesus and His message. In daily living, people are being prepared, given wisdom, led to action, and seeing the good results of their obedience. The good news is spreading, and people are receiving forgiveness.

When we see this evidence of the Holy Spirit, can we exchange our will for God's will? Can we recognize Him as the center of life? If we trust God, we will be able to exhibit the vitality and overwhelming joy the world needs to see. I invite you to rejoice.

December 2017

The Secret to Contentment

I asked God, "How come I'm never satisfied?" No matter how good I have it, I appreciate the goodness for only a time. Then I want something more, somewhere else. I think, *The grass is greener over there*. I am tired of repeatedly wanting. I asked God, "Why am I like this? Why can't I just enjoy what I have and where I am?" I'm talking about my struggle to find quiet peace. God promises us in Psalm 91:1 (NIV) that if we stick to Him as if we were affixed with superglue, then His shadow will be our resting place. That's what I want: God as my frontman, and I get to rest in the coolness of His shadow.

We can find the best rest in God. Other sources only help temporarily. We can put money toward buying happiness, but there is never enough money. We can sleep at night, but morning comes too soon. We can be awake and numbed, but let's not stupefy ourselves. Sleepwalking is no way to spend our days. We can enjoy being alive. When I'm fully awake, I enjoy the beauty of colors, the wonder of birds flying, and the friendliness of people. I know that at this point, I am where God has placed me. But I still question, "Is this all there is?" Questions like that are not from God. I now recognize them as the sneaky *voice of discontent* whose aim is to distract and discourage me.

I have wisdom now. Last Sunday, I visited Woodburn Foursquare Church. God used Pastor Luis to answer my question. I am now prepared. When the lying voice tries to say that life is passing me by or I'm never going to accomplish anything great in my life, I know how I can shut it up. Pastor Luis encouraged his listeners to take a stand for contentment. He used examples from Paul's life. Paul's life is highly useful for teaching us how to gain contentment amid the struggles of life. In his travels, Paul was shipwrecked three times, five times whipped, beaten with rods three times, stoned, spent a night and day in the open sea, went hungry, thirsty, cold. He faced death again and again. At the end of his life, he shared the insight he gained from his troubles. In Philippians 4:12 (NIV), he says he learned the secret of being content in any and every situation. I can get grumpy when I'm hungry, but Paul didn't let circumstances affect his contentment.

If you drew a circle on a piece of paper, representing your life, what would be in the center? Who or what does everything in your life revolve around? For me, Pastor Luis' sermon was a helpful reminder that it's all about Jesus. On the one side of life, there's a trap set for us, but we are safe when we focus on the one who promises a good life and His ever-present help in troubling times. Paul could stay content because he had learned God gave him strength. The secret to contentment is knowing our strength is from God. God is our power spot. Focus on Jesus.

August 2018

In the Communion

Are you in the communion? Holy Spirit told me three mornings in a row, just as I was waking up, "You are in the communion." I have wondered what that means since the late 1980s. Jesus instituted the first communion just before His crucifixion, but I'm not headed for physical death. Paul told the Romans we have already died, been buried, and raised to new life in Christ (Romans 6:3–4, NIV). What is it about the crucifixion? Being daily crucified with Jesus is being up close to His emotions, spiritual struggle, ultimate victory. That is intimacy with Jesus. See also in Galatians

> I have been crucified in Christ and I no longer live, but Christ lives in me. The life I know live in the body, I live by faith in the Son of God, who loved me and gave himself for me.
>
> Galatians 2:20 (NIV)

Being in the communion is intimacy, community, bread and wine, spiritual belonging, and service. Jesus told us to re-member Him. Could that mean before we come together, we are Jesus' body dismembered, and in communion, He is re-membered? What happens in that re-membering? There's a connection between community and communion.

The Trinity is an example of community. Father and Son commune with each other. Jesus explains, in John 12:50 (NIV), that He only says what the Father tells Him to say. In Mark 1:2 (NIV), there's an encouraging word from the Father to Jesus. God is one but also a community of three. We are part of that community as well

> My Father's house has many rooms; if that were not so, would I have told you that I am going there to prepare a place for you? And if I go and prepare a place for you, I will come back and take you to be with me that you also may be where I am.
>
> John 14:2–3 (NIV)

Holy Spirit, Jesus, and the Father live inside us. We are in Christ. Consider this, the richness of 1 Corinthians 2:10 (NIV) includes: Holy Spirit shares with us the deep things of God.

What is a deep thing of God? How about that God prepares us to labor with Him (1 Corinthians 3:9, NIV)? Mark 2:22 (NIV) says new wine needs to be put in new wineskins. Old wineskins could not bear the pressure of the fermentation and maturation of new wine. If we want the new wine of being anointed and used, we need to be new wineskins. Pliable and current. "Pliable" means we can ditch our plans and obey God. Able to work as a body, built up in Christ. Being "current" means we must hear God's voice today.

Oswald Chambers says we are grapes. This reminds me of being on the vine. We need to be crushed so we can be poured out to serve others. In Philippians 2:17 (NIV), Paul told about his being poured out. Chambers says there's a "broken bread and poured out wine aspect of life."[23] Yes. As a believer, you are in the communion. What part of the body are you? If you are being crushed, can you see yourself as being made ready for God's use?

Prayer

In the same way the Spirit [comes to us and] helps us in our weakness. We do not know what prayer to offer *or* how to offer it as we should, but the Spirit Himself [knows our need and at the right time] intercedes on our behalf with sighs *and* groanings too deep for words.

Romans 8:26 (AMP)

Small Actions Can Have Big Results

She's a mom, but that's not why she's on my mind. I keep thinking about her son and the difficulty I am having in keeping my promise. I met her because she's one of my customers. Sometimes she pays her utility bill by sending a check. I see her when she pays it in person. She pays for it at my counter. Each time I see her, we only talk for a minute. It doesn't take long to pay a bill.

The first couple of times she came in, she told me her son was in Iraq. She is proud of him, scared for him, and prays for his safety and well-being. I believe we, as a people, can empathize with her. It was different during the Vietnam War. Then, the soldiers got lumped in with the war. If a person was anti-war, then they were anti-soldier too. Now we are making the distinction. A person can be anti-war but still support the men and women who are in harm's way.

After a couple of months, she noticed a picture I had by my computer. In the picture, a row of fourteen German shepherds sits perfectly still while a cat saunters by in front of them. The verse at the bottom of the picture is from Psalm 23:4 (KJV), which says, "Yea, though I walk through the valley of the shadow of death, I will fear no evil." She not only noticed the picture, but she told me her son would appreciate it as well. She was going to describe it to him. I did her one better than that. I gave her a photocopy of the picture. I am so glad I had a copy of it handy. She was pleased.

The story continued a couple of months later when she came to pay her bill. She told me her son really likes the picture. His buddies like the picture. The picture is hanging in their tent. It touched me that a small gesture on my part could be so encouraging and helpful. I feel connected, now, to her son and his buddies. I feel more involved with their struggles. That's why I feel bad about not keeping my promise. I made my promise after reading an email about Winston Churchill. During World War II, Prime Minister Churchill asked Englanders to pray every day at 6:00 p.m. for the country's soldiers.

For a minute or two every day at six o'clock.

I agree with the principle of praying together. To those who love and obey Him, God says. "Five of you will chase a hundred, and a hundred of you will chase ten thousand" (Leviticus 26:8, NIV). The email invited folks on the east coast to pray at three o'clock. On the west coast, we pray at six o'clock. The people in the time zones between the east and west pray according to their zones. I decided to do it, and I sent the email to others asking them to do it. It is a powerful idea. Don't you think so? The trouble is I never notice when it's six o'clock. I usually notice the time after the day has flown by. It's way past six, and I'm home. I've been wondering how I can notice it's six o'clock. If I notice it's six, then I can remember to pray. One idea: I could get a watch with an alarm feature and set it for six. But that won't work. Trust me. Watches break on me.

Here's my request. I'm requesting on behalf of our country's soldiers. Would you join us in prayer every day at six? And then, if you see a middle-aged woman nearby, would you tell her it's 6:00 p.m.? Maybe she won't know what you're talking about. It's your choice whether or not to tell her what we're up to.

On the other hand, maybe the woman will be me. If it's me, you will be helping me keep my promise. I'll thank you.

May 2007

God Does Not Forget

It's true. God does answer prayers. Have you heard that God answers *yes, no, or not yet?* For example, a *yes* is guaranteed if your request is for Him to forgive your sins and enter your heart. Acts 16:31 (NIV) says, "Believe in the Lord Jesus and you will be saved." I wasn't really sure God existed when I gave myself to Him. I said, "If you're there, I need you. Forgive my sins. Come into my life." I had some reservations but enough belief to ask. God answered with a yes. Thirty-five years later, I am still grateful for that yes.

The Bible does offer an understanding of why we sometimes get no for an answer, but I want to share about God answering me with *not yet.* Last week I was cleaning out some files, getting rid of old tax filings and appliance warranty cards. I found a journal from years ago in which I had recorded my desires, dreams, and prayers. The first entry is a newspaper article about a writers' conference. The article is glued into the journal and is followed by my feelings. I wanted to go to the conference. It fit with my desire to tell people about God's goodness. I couldn't go, though. My husband, Gilbert, and I did not have the $250 required for attendance. Gilbert was sorry I couldn't go. I was disappointed and somewhat resentful.

In my journal, I wrote,

Dear God, I confess to you my feelings of resentment and ask for your forgiveness. I know, Lord, that you can provide for me if you want me at this conference. Thank you, in faith, I say this, for your forgiveness. In Jesus' name. Amen.

After writing down my prayer, I wrote

Well, we don't have the $. But I believe God is going to provide for me. Last night, while discussing with

Gilbert, I felt like this was a ripe opportunity to trust God. I place this need/situation/my desire to GO in God's hands.

The next thing I recorded in my journal:

This morning, while waking up, I heard a kind, manly voice say, "I like/appreciate/enjoy Chicken Soup for the Soul stories and I know you do too. What kind of style will your writing have?" I answered, "Encouraging," and then I felt like that didn't answer the question right because "encouraging" is not a style, but before I could explain myself, I woke up. I understand this interaction to be an encouragement from God. He's teaching me lately about trust and dependence on Him and letting go of control. This is an opportunity to do that.

According to my journal, this all happened eight years ago. I've shortened my story a little, but you get the idea. I said, "Please, God." He said, "OK, but not right now."

Eight years later, I am writing for the *Woodburn Independent*. I hope my columns are encouraging to you. My eight-year wait was not hard because I forgot I even wanted to write. In fact, after a few entries about writing. My journal entries changed focus. I got interested in charter schools. But God did not forget. Therefore, be encouraged. God answers prayers. If He answers *not yet*, He won't forget. He's faithful.

August 2007

Necessity of Prayer

When a person prospects for gold, sometimes it is found in streams. Other times, the gold is dug out of the ground. A miner who digs it out will try to follow a vein of gold to the mother lode. Just like gold, spiritual treasure sometimes requires us to dig for it. We follow hints and insights. We seek wisdom. We try to find the door of knowledge so we can open it and get understanding.

Recently, I've spent time reflecting and appreciating. I'd like to share my thoughts with you. Together we can give shape and form to the hints of beauty I've gathered. Are you with me? Here we go.

I picked up the book, *The Best Spiritual Writing of 1999* by Philip Zaleski. I read several poems and one person's spiritual autobiography. Reading them put me in a special, quiet place. When I checked the book out of the library, I had not expected to be transported. I was just curious about what qualified as the "best spiritual writing." But I was transported. I felt like the writers shared God with me, and I had been to a holy place. I was inspired to dig for more.

Being hungry for more, I was ready to receive when I came across this quote, often attributed to Jonas Salk, "What we think of as the moment of discovery is really the discovery of the right question." In other words, the answer is in the question. The question is necessary to see the answer. Just like having a goal is necessary to achievement. When there's no target, we are just shooting into the air.

The importance of having a question resonates with my experience. Remember last month when I told you about my receiving a timely answer to prayer? I shared,

> I remember another instance of God's care... I was going through an emotional time... I was hurting. In my distress, I started pacing back and forth ... I was crying and shot out a distress call to God, 'Help me!' Just then, that very moment, there was a knock on my door. It was a UPS deliveryman. His delivery was a present from a friend of mine in Georgia. She sent me a framed handkerchief.

It was beautiful. Her accompanying letter was full of love and encouragement. The timing of her gift was perfect - it was just what I needed. Please notice: my friend Bonnie could not have timed her present to reach me at my point of greatest need. That was God.

Now I'm asking, would I have received Bonnie's gift as God's love in a tangible form if I had not been crying for God's help? If I had not been seeking God so ardently, would I have recognized His presence? If we drink from the stream, but are not looking for the gold flecks, will we find the treasure? Doesn't this point out the importance of seeking God?

Let's be clear. I'm not saying, ask and then accept anything that comes along as an answer from God. Don't let your asking set you up for accepting something that is not from God. I'm saying, if you ask God a question or seek God, then you'll be available to perceive His response/ His presence. Consider the time I asked God a question, and a couple of days later, a young man came into the restaurant where I was working with my answer. He was wearing a t-shirt with a Bible verse on it. The verse answered my question. If I had not asked the question, would I have noticed God's love toward me?

It looks like our seeking God is part of the process of Him showing Himself to us. That's why prayer is necessary. God knows what we need before we ask, but when we ask, then we are primed to see His love for us when He answers. I am glad that God shows Himself to us the way He does. In church this morning, Pastor Joseph talked about the prophet Isaiah. God visited this holy man. You can read Isaiah's response in Isaiah 6:8; 11 (NIV) "And I said, 'Here I am. Send me!'... Then I said, 'For how long, Lord?'" He was blown away. Emotionally undone. His experience was that the holy was visiting the hopeless. He was overwhelmed by God's divinity and his own uncleanness.

Direct encounters with the holy bring to light our need for cleansing. That is why I appreciate that when God visits, He usually wears a cloak. I am not put face to face with my neediness. Instead, I can snuggle into Him and enjoy His love. Thank you for accompanying me on this prospecting adventure. I invite you to continue asking and seeking. If you ask, you will receive. If you seek, you will find.

November 2007

What Is Prayer?

My brother and sister-in-law are part of a Relay For Life event in Southern California. Their team from church gets to share a handout with the rest of the event's participants, so my brother asked me for a page on prayer. Here is what I gave him.

What I Know about Prayer

- ☐ God hears all prayers.
- ☐ God wants us to pray because He wants to be in a relationship with us.
- ☐ God wants us to pray so He can answer our prayers and show His love for us.
- ☐ God wants us to pray so we can see Him in action and give Him the glory.
- ☐ God wants us to lean on Him in prayer, to depend on Him, to trust Him.
- ☐ God wants us to pray so we will take our eyes off the problem and put them on the problem solver.
- ☐ God wants us to pray as a testimony to others.
- ☐ God wants us to pray so that we can leave the situation in His hands and have His peace.
- ☐ God wants us to pray so we will hear Him when He's speaking to us.
- ☐ God uses our prayer time to give us encouragement, guidance, and glimpses of His being in our life.
- ☐ Developing a consistent prayer life takes time. (I wonder if it takes a lifetime.)
- ☐ My biggest problem in prayer is getting distracted by other

thoughts. When a stray thought comes through my mind, sometimes it helps to add it to my prayer.

☐ Reading the Psalms enriches my prayers.

☐ I can pray better when I'm walking - rather than sitting still.

☐ Sometimes, sitting quietly in a place of prayer like a church helps me pray.

☐ Reading about great men and women of God encourages me to pray.

☐ Some people use praise and worship music to help them pray.

☐ Sometimes, I have no words, and all I can do is cry in God's direction.

☐ When I don't know what to pray, the Spirit sometimes prays through me. (Romans 8:26)

☐ Praying with someone has helped me reach out to God.

☐ Praying is just talking to God as if He were right next to me.

☐ Praying for someone is a double blessing: I get to spend time with God and give someone a gift.

☐ Praying for someone or a situation is a blessing because I get to partner with God to effect change.

☐ Jesus prays for us. (Hebrews 7:25)

☐ I hope I never stop praying.

Someone told me if I want to pray without ceasing, then I should develop the habit of having all my thoughts be a conversation with God. Instead of talking to myself, talk to God. I think this is a worthwhile endeavor. I am trying to do it. We will always have prayer. When God answers our prayers for a cure for cancers, we will no longer need Relay For Life events. In the name of Jesus, amen.

April 2008

Prayers Do Not Have to Be Fancy

As persons of faith, we cannot help but be encouraged. Can we? We know that God hears even the shortest, most informal prayers. We know He has power over death. When I read the following story, I thought of sharing it with you. It's entitled, "A Miracle of the Heart"

Doug* was a frequent patient in the Emergency department at Tillamook County General Hospital. On one particular day, he was blue, gasping for breath and his eyes were sunken.

To Larry Hamilton, registered nurse and director of the Emergency department, it appeared the end was near for Doug. As requested by the attending physician and internist, Hamilton was preparing to administer morphine to ensure Doug was comfortable.

"As I was leaving to go and retrieve the medication, Doug reached out and grabbed my arm," Hamilton recalls. "He had panic in his eyes. His breathing was so labored he could hardly speak. Mustering all his remaining strength, he gasped, 'Please, please.' I looked into his terrified eyes and simply said, 'Doug, heaven is not a bad place.'"

His grip tightened, and between gasps, he replied, "I am not ready!"

Hamilton stood for a moment looking at Doug. Then, glancing toward the ceiling, he simply said, "God, You hear this man's prayer," and turned to get the morphine.

The day was busy and there were many patients in the Emergency department. As Hamilton passed another bed on his way to get Doug's medication, the nurse caring for that patient grabbed him. The patient had developed a lethal heart rhythm and needed immediate intervention. Modern medicine did its work, and in about twenty minutes the patient was out of danger.

Soon, it dawned on Hamilton he had left Doug in distress and had done nothing to relieve his pain or suffering. He ran to the medication room and retrieved Doug's morphine. Slipping back into the man's curtain, Hamilton was shocked when he saw Doug sitting there with a big smile on his face.

171

"Hello, Larry!" he said. "I feel great!"

All Hamilton could do was gasp. "Doug, did someone give you a treatment?' he asked.

"No", Doug replied. "You said something just before you left, and I suddenly felt better."

He took a deep breath to demonstrate his new ability to breathe. A chill ran down Hamilton's back as it dawned on him that a miracle had just taken place.

Hamilton wanted to visit Doug and share Jesus with him, but circumstances just never seemed right. However, during one of Doug's later hospital stays, a Faith in Action community volunteer did have that opportunity, and Doug gave his heart to God.

Doug did not have his health restored, but it became obvious his heart was healed. Just before he died, Doug was being transferred to a care center via ambulance and Hamilton overheard him telling his story to a young paramedic who had not yet met Jesus.

Names have been changed to protect patient privacy.[24]

This story demonstrates God's loving nature. And we see that prayers don't have to be fancy. Sometimes I just pray His name. Jesus. Jesus. Jesus.

March 2010

Protection

Because he set his love on Me, therefore I will save him; I will set him [securely] on high, because he knows My name [he confidently trusts and relies on Me, knowing I will never abandon him, no, never]. He will call upon Me, and I will answer him; I will be with him in trouble; I will rescue him and honor him.

Psalm 91:14–15 (AMP)

Who Do You Claim?

When things go really wrong, who do you call? Ghostbusters? The "good hands" people? God?

My teenage son and his friend, Rico, found themselves in a situation. I'll let Rico tell it: "Dillon and I were at the market buying some burritos and stuff because we were hungry. I was wearing a red t-shirt and Dillon was wearing a red hat. Some guys came up to us. It seemed like they wanted to fight. They asked us, 'What do you claim? *What do you claim?*' Dillon said, 'Jesus. We claim Jesus.' The guy said, 'What the—' Just then my two brothers showed up. The guys went away and left us alone."

At this point, I will re-phrase the question. Instead of "Who do you call?" I'll ask you, "Who do you bring to the fight?" Yesterday I was doing errands and had to walk around a group of four young boys to enter one establishment. The oldest was probably fourteen years old. It was immediately clear they were challenging each other, two against two. They exchanged the same taunt back and forth. It went something like "Oh yeah? I'm going to bring..." and they would give a name. They were posturing regarding the strength they could bring to a fight. They were bragging about their strength based on who they were connected to.

In his book, *Angels: God's Secret Agents*, the Reverend Billy Graham tells the story of a woman missionary in China who brought God to the fight. She had that connection. Her name was Miss Monsen. Her mission compound sheltered hundreds of women and children. One night, bandits surrounded the compound intending to break down the gates and loot whatever they found. It was a scary time. The missionary was up all night praying and encouraging others to pray and trust God. Graham reports,

> Though fearful things happened all around, the bandits left the mission compound untouched. In the morning, people from

three different neighborhood families asked Miss Monsen, "Who were those four people, three sitting and one standing, quietly watching from the top of your house all night long?" When she told them that no one had been on the housetop, they refused to believe her, saying, "We saw them with our own eyes!" She then told them that God still sent angels to guard His children in their hour of danger.[25]

God takes care of His children. And He is not limited. Consider Daniel's experience. Daniel's story is an old one, but still good. As a member of the king's staff, Daniel performed his duties so exceptionally that the king was considering making him the number one man. Everyone except the king would be under Daniel. Of course, the other king's men did not like this. They were probably jealous. They plotted to get rid of Daniel. Because they couldn't find anything wrong with his governing, they figured the only way to get him was if praying to God was illegal. Daniel loved and trusted in God. He prayed three times a day.

They made it happen. The plotting men tricked the king into writing a law that people could only revere the king; they could not pray to God. If someone was found praying to God, they would be thrown into the lions' pit. The law was made. Daniel prayed. The men accused him. The king couldn't excuse him. Daniel ended up surrounded by hungry lions. All night. I have never been in such danger, but if I ever was, I know who I'd be praying to! In the morning, the king anxiously returned to the lions' pit to see if Daniel's God had protected him. He had. Daniel reported, "My God sent his angel, and he shut the mouths of the lions. They have not hurt me" (Daniel 6:12, NIV).

God is not limited. He can save us wherever we are, even in the bottom of a pit. Death can be surrounding us, staring us in the face. We can survive it. God is that good. Those who opposed Daniel did not fare as well. After the king pulled Daniel out of the pit, he threw

Daniel's enemies into the pit. Daniel 6:24 (NIV) says, "And before they reached the floor of the den, the lions overpowered them and crushed all their bones." That's gruesome, but it does underline the importance of knowing who to call on when things go really wrong.

July 2007

When Bad Happens, God Is with Us

When the sun is out, it shines on the good and the bad among us. When it rains, it falls on the just and the unjust. No one is spared having problems. The question is, when bad things happen, where is God? There are several possible approaches to this question. They are each worth considering. I hope you bear with me because I have something wonderful to share.

Approach number one: By the very fact that God is God, we can know He is in the midst of our problems. God is all-knowing, all love, and present everywhere. God is perfect. If your idea of God has Him being less than perfect, then I ask you, "What are you comparing Him to?" If you have a *Being B* who is more loving than *Being A*, then *Being B* is God. Do you see? That one whom you use as a measure, He is God. Therefore, since God is perfect and everywhere, He is also in the middle of your problem. Smack dab in it with you.

Approach number two: God told us He would always be with us. He is not like men. He does not lie. Therefore, we can believe Him. Jesus told His followers, "I am with you always, even to the end of the world" (Matthew 28:20, LB). When you're going through trials, take your eyes off your situation and look at Jesus.

Approach number three: Remember, we are looking at a question that comes up every day. Sometimes people ask it with a high-pitched wail of agony. Other times, tired defeat wonders, "Where is God?" In our problems, we want to know if God is available. Does He know what's happening to me? Does He care? Yes. The answer is yes.

You may have agreed mentally with the logic of *approach one*. You may be hoping in your heart that you can trust the word of *approach two*. *Approach three* is the wonderfulness I promised you. It is a recent experience of God's availability, knowledge, and love. We can make no other sense of it: God is with us.

Let's look at approach three's answer to, "When bad things happen. where is God?" Here's the bad. A bridge collapsed into the

Mississippi River last month in St. Paul, Minnesota. The bridge is a major route of travel. When I first heard about its collapse, I wondered if it was an act of terrorism. It wasn't. Nevertheless, taking down such a bridge would be an effective way of killing lots of people. Sadly, some did die because the rain does fall on the just and the unjust. But *lots* of people did not die that day. God intervened.

As reported by Aimee Herd, God's grace and protection were there.

> Due to the construction on the bridge, the traffic was not at the normally full flow, or speed… And then the school bus, filled with fifty children that rode the concrete on the way down during the collapse, didn't tip over—all the children were saved.[26]

Ms. Herd's article continues with a young man's report of God's protection. The young man, Matthew, says,

> "I was coming home to take a shower, and then pick up my friend across the I 35 W. bridge… I was headed into the city … it was bumper-to-bumper. I was praying and talking to the Lord, and the next minute the Lord gave me this vision. In the vision [the bridge was] shaking—it started to snap and broke through. I saw two cars go off the edge into the Mississippi. Then, [after the vision], I said, 'What is that all about Lord? You need to talk to me.' God told me to '*Stop!*'" (I was 100 feet away from the bridge) "He said, 'You need to stop right there.' I said, 'Lord, there are cars behind me,' (There were about 100 people in the line of traffic behind him, and many had begun honking their horns at him). "But God said, 'That's okay, you need to stop. So I stopped. And then the Lord said, 'Look.' People were going around me—about 20 feet away from the bridge. That's when it snapped—[the bridge] broke down and crashed. I saw 2 cars go off the bridge, and I was like … 'wow!' At first I was sitting in the car waiting, thanking the Lord, because it could've been me on that bridge. Then people came up to me and said, 'Thank you.' I got out and looked from the side [at

the collapse]...It was traumatic seeing what happened. And then the police told me to go back in my car and turn around."[27]

Where was God when the bridge was collapsing? He was right there. Is something collapsing in your life? Reach out. God is right there.

September 2007

God Has Never Let Me Down

When it comes to flavors, do you like vanilla or chocolate better? I love chocolate. Have you ever had a wonderfully rich piece of chocolate? I remember my first piece of Godiva chocolate. Having that chocolate was a life-affecting experience that opened my eyes.

To explain, I need to back up my story. I grew up in a middle-class household. We were not hurting, but we were not surrounded by luxuries either. When, in college, a friend gave me Godiva chocolates, it was a super birthday present. Not only was the chocolate better than my favorite peanut M&Ms, but tasting it introduced me to a world of luxury. It was a peek at another level of life. It was a signpost toward a world larger than I knew. Now I should find that friend from thirty years ago and thank her again for those chocolates! What if she had not given them to me? What if no one had ever introduced me to extravagant luxury? How would I see my world? I am thankful she introduced me to luxury. I believe she knew she had a good thing, and she wanted to share it with me, her friend. Isn't that what we do when we find a good restaurant, a good movie, an attractive outfit on sale? We tell our friends. We share the goodness.

What I wish is that I could share with everyone the goodness I have discovered. When I find something worthwhile, I want everyone else to have it too. That is why I am so thrilled to be writing to you. Every month, I get to share about God's availability and goodness. Thank you for listening. What I want to tell you today: God has never let me down. I've been a Christian for over thirty-five years. He's been faithful to me for more than three decades.

I remember one late-night walk I took when I lived in Santa Barbara. I was restless at home, so I walked down to the cliff. There was a full moon, and its path of light came across the ocean water straight to me. I enjoyed the beauty of the evening and ended up strolling through the park, along the cliff's edge. I did not think anything of it when two young men were walking together toward me. I was innocent then. When the three of us were within speaking distance, I said, "Good evening." I don't remember them saying anything to me, but I overheard one of them say to the other, "See? We should have." The other one answered, "No." That's all I needed to hear. I immediately changed from a stroll to a brisk walk and cut across the park toward home. When I look back on that, I see God's protection over me. I was alone. I was behaving naively toward them, and yet something, someone, stopped those two young men from doing whatever it was they were looking to do to someone.

I remember another instance of God's care. I was battling my thoughts. The war started when I was feeling personally accomplished, then prideful, then flirtatious. I thought I was having a friendly conversation, but the line between friendly and flirting can be razor-thin. Thoughts about the one-with-whom-I'd-flirted came to mind unbidden and unwelcome. They were distracting and condemning. I felt trapped. I confessed my pride and self-absorption to God, and He forgave me. Hallelujah. The thoughts persisted.

I tried praying for the man and his family, reasoning that if Satan saw me praying for them, his plan would backfire, and he would stop harassing me. The condemnation continued. I finally told my husband about my struggle. That was hard to do. He counseled me to cease all friendly conversation with the man. My husband prayed for me.

After several weeks of soul torment, I finally accepted God's forgiveness and deliverance. I was watching late-night television, and Pastor Perry Stone came on. He explained what had happened to me. A fiery dart had struck me. I needed to strengthen my shield with water and oil; strengthen my faith with the cleansing of God's Word and the anointing of the Holy Spirit. I went to sleep that night, knowing God had given me personal instructions.

The next morning, my husband Gilbert told me, "You are free. Because of the blood." Gilbert didn't even say, "Good morning." He calmly stated the facts of my freedom. Then I remembered God's waking me up the previous week with the phrase, "The thirteenth amendment." I researched the thirteenth amendment and discovered it is the one that abolished slavery.

Before God gave me that wonderful news, He had begun pointing out red cars and trucks on the road. I would be driving, and I would notice, with happiness, a red car or truck. This went on for days until I asked God if He was saying something to me. At the moment of my asking, I saw three red cars in a row, and I heard in my spirit, "There's power in the blood of Jesus." I became serious about personally applying the blood to every situation, person, resource, and relationship.

Now, dear reader, we go back to the morning of Gilbert's speaking God's word of my freedom. That morning in church, Pastor Max preached on Galatians 5:1 (NIV), "It is for freedom that Christ has set us free. Stand firm, then, and do not let yourself be burdened again by a yoke of slavery" and John 8:36 (NIV) "So if the Son sets you free, you are freed indeed," both about our freedom. Christ set us free. Pastor Max told us not to fall back into sin. Jesus says we really are free. We must believe this to our core, practice it, and live it out. Let it inform our behavior so that we can testify to others.

Bottom line: The devil has been overcome. We are free in Christ. Tell someone.

God Is Involved in the Details

I feel loved. Recently, I experienced God's care in a way that left me feeling good all day. I want you to know God is involved in the details of your life. He is watchful. Don't worry, for he is right there with you.

To set the scene for you: I help the pastor lead worship on Sunday mornings. I stand up front and sing into the microphone. I stand slightly behind the amplifying speaker because I get nervous up there. The speaker gives me a little covering.

Recently, a church in Idaho invited the pastor and his wife to minister to them on a Sunday morning. That meant I was asked to do more than help the pastor lead worship. I was asked to lead it all by myself. This made me even more nervous, but I had a day's notice, so I took the time to prepare myself. I wanted to be in a good place, as close as ever, with God because leading worship by remote control doesn't work. The leader has to be in tune. Just as a musical instrument, I was called upon to be an instrument of praise and worship.

I trust you have an idea of what I was experiencing. I felt responsible and nervous. When I awoke that Sunday morning, I immediately became upset. Thoughts about a certain credit agency, which is harassing me, bulleted my consciousness. This agency has not listened to my husband's and my explanations that we paid that loan. We no longer owe that money. They have been so relentless, and I have gotten so frustrated, I have even considered writing a column about them, advising you all to steer clear of them. With these thought bullets hitting my brain, I started to get distracted from my goal of being in tune with God. I finally chose to let go of my frustration. I asked God to take care of the whole credit agency situation.

No sooner did I have peace of mind then, *bam*! I started thinking about a certain family member and how I disagreed with something they'd been doing recently. I started to feel helpless and frustrated. I realized I needed to let go of those thoughts just like I had the previous barrage. I thought of turning on some Christian music to lift my mood. I dismissed the idea as it would take too much effort to do. I decided to get out of bed and get ready for the day. As part of my getting ready, I went out to the truck to turn it on. I sat in the truck for the seven minutes it needed to warm up, but my mood had not improved. The only prayer I could manage was to focus on Jesus.

When I came back into the house, Christian music was playing. It was just what I needed. To hear the music helped focus me on God. When my husband told me why he had turned it on, then I was really blessed. Gilbert, my husband, said that while he made pancakes for our son's breakfast, he understood God to tell him, "She's outside in the truck. Before she comes in, have some music on." I believe Gilbert heard from God. I trust his relationship with God. And what he did exactly fit my need. I also believe God was with me in my struggle. He cares about me. He saw my battle and extended His love to me.

The worship time that morning was a blessed time. I wasn't alone up there, after all. My husband volunteered to sing with me, and I had the fresh assurance that God cares. He loves us.

May 2009

God Sees the Big Picture

God knows how much money you have in your wallet, and He knows how you feel about that money.

I was stressing about what to do. I heard the prophets say a national and then global financial shaking and collapse might happen in a matter of weeks. I was asking God what He wanted me to do. Should I prepare? What was His wisdom? I didn't hear any clear directives, but I felt all right about using my Saturday morning to buy extra food and water and withdraw $100 from my checking account. I put the groceries away in a place apart from the rest of our food. I told my son not to eat that food until I said so. I couldn't decide whether to put the money with the groceries or put it in my jewelry box. Therefore, the money was still in my purse the following morning at church.

During testimony time at church, a man stood up and said God had asked him if he would rather be comfortable or obedient. God told him to quit his job. God had another job for him as a youth pastor. This man and his wife decided to say "Yes" to God. Even though it was hard, they had a little baby, and they were just getting established. Now he's without a job and looking for a job as a youth pastor. He has an interview soon in another state, between him and one other candidate. He's hopeful. God's been providing for them all along. Even though he's unemployed, God has met their needs.

While he was sharing his story, God told me to give him the $100 I had in my purse. I know God's voice, but I still questioned, "Is this you, God, or is it just my compassion for his story?" God told me I'd be feeding His ministry. I knew that if I left church that morning without giving the man my $100, I would feel bad. I would feel like I'd missed an opportunity to be obedient. Been there, done that.

After church, I went up to the man and said, "God bless you." He said, "God bless you." He meant it. I could tell he wasn't parroting me. Even while he was saying it, I had my hand out to shake his hand. I gave him a Pentecostal handshake, turned, and walked away. I felt peace.

I got in my car to drive home, and before I could turn the key in the ignition, God told me, "Now your money is safe with me." Wow! The goodness of God. He knows my fears, needs, and how best to take care of me. I was so happy to hear God say He is taking care of my money from now on that I thought, *Maybe I should give that man some more money!*

When God speaks, do you want to be comfortable or obedient?

Dear Reader, before submitting this book for publication, I checked back with the church where these blessings happened. They updated me regarding the couple who left their place of comfort in order to be obedient. The young father did get hired for the position of youth pastor, and more recently, the couple has been pastoring a church. God takes care of His children.

God Is Not Done

Do you prefer fast-paced action movies or romantic comedies? Because my husband enjoys the former and I prefer movies that have happy endings, he often goes to movies without me. But lately, we've been going to the theater together. Hollywood offerings have been such a blessing! We saw *Heaven Is for Real*. Yes, it is! We saw *God's Not Dead*. Have you seen it yet? The other day I unintentionally renamed it *God's Not Done*. I was talking about the movie, and my hope in God showed itself: God will never quit or change His mind about us. His love is forever. What He says about Himself is that He is the same yesterday, today, and forever.

So, how was He yesterday? My friend Carolyne shared with me the beginnings of her autobiography. She's seventy-three years old and has had many yesterdays evidencing God's goodness. He's her healer, guide, and protection. On a hunting trip, God let her see His protection detail.

Carolyne's Story

About 2009–2010, my daughter, son, and some others had a run-in with men running bear with dogs out of season. Later, we learned someone had turned them in. I was worried they might think we had, so before my daughter and I went out again, I asked our church to pray for our safety. I knew God would take care of us. Our church sent us with a prayer cloth and holy oil.

We were slowly driving, looking for deer to hunt, when the poachers passed us, looking hard at our pickup. That seemed odd at the time. The last place we stopped was a meadow. I was sitting on a log, my daughter Robbin to my left when I saw movement to our right. Then I glimpsed another movement. I couldn't understand how two men could come that close, and we didn't hear them. Then I understood they were angels there to protect us. One was holding a large scythe and the other a large staff. These were their weapons.

191

They were in hunting camouflage clothes.

My daughter wanted to know what I was looking so hard at. I told her if they attacked, she wouldn't need her gun. We had angels protecting us. She wanted to know where they were, what they wore, what they looked like, and if they had weapons. I told her. She seems to know when something is about to happen out of the ordinary. We hunted awhile longer and left for home. I told her they were probably in the back of the pickup when the poachers' vehicle passed us. I thank God for His protection.

I trust my friend is telling me the truth. Angels are real, God does care about every detail of our days, and He answers prayers.

May 2014

Fire!

I ran and ran, yelling, "Fire!" It was not a dream. It was the fourth of July.

Earlier in the day, I prayed for God's protection for our property because we were coming home late, and I would not be there to guard against fireworks danger. I depend on God. He takes care of me. My praying done, Gilbert and I went to a friends' barbecue in Salem, a delicious potluck. Children played on the trampoline. We had a good time visiting, taking pictures. We were going to wait until dark to do the fireworks, but after starting with the poppers, we continued with the rest early. Just after dusk, we left for home.

When we got home, it was totally dark. Our neighbors' fireworks were thrilling. After watching for a while, I wanted to check on the cat. She doesn't like loud noises. I was in the backyard calling her name when I saw flames. The neighbor's tool shed was catching on fire!

"Fire!" I ran through the backyard, into the house, out the front door, over to the neighbor's driveway. "Fire! Fire! Fire!" I did not stop running, and I kept yelling! Gilbert was yelling at me, "Suzanne! Where?" He took off his jacket, prepared to fight flames. Our neighbors ceased their fireworks and hurried to their backyard. After they saved their shed, they came back and thanked me. My husband and I stayed in our backyard for another hour, on fire watch. But there was no more drama that night.

I thank God for taking care of our property and neighborhood. All of our houses are close together. My neighbor's tool shed could have been only the first domino to burn. God worked out the timing of our coming home earlier than we had planned. He sent me to the backyard. It happens that way. I think I'm going for the cat and God has me fighting fires! One more point: He doesn't always answer as quickly as I want, but He's never, never late. My property doesn't even have the smell of smoke.

I have a question for God. When I prayed earlier that day, I prayed in English and then, with no forethought, prayed in tongues. What did I pray? For the timing to be perfect? For my being able to feel a nudge? That I would respond immediately to His nudge? Praying in my heavenly language felt like confirmation my prayer was heard and answered in the affirmative. Was I already praising God for what He was going to do?

I am still praising God today. We serve a big God.

July 2019

Epilogue

Dear Reader,

Upon near completion, I asked God if there was anything else to include in this book. He reminded me of the following article on authority and power that I wrote years ago in obedience to a divine nudge. I haven't yet submitted it as a column for the newspaper. I pray that you will take to heart God's call on your life. Lives depend on it. In Jesus' name, amen.

Consider David's triumph over the giant. David said to the Philistine,

> You come against me with sword and spear and javelin, but I come against you in the name of the Lord Almighty, the God of the armies of Israel, whom you have defied. This day the Lord will hand you over to me, and I'll strike you down and cut off your head.
>
> 1 Samuel 17:45–46 (NIV)

Authority and Power

We have the assignment to point people to Jesus. To share the gospel and talk about the cross. It's a life and death assignment. Thank God that He works in and through us. Here's a true story.

My friend George works in the Information Systems department for the city of Woodburn. As part of his work, he gets called to fix computer problems for all the city's departments, including the police department. Working with the police department, he became close friends with the officers. When an officer died in the line of duty, the other police officers acknowledged George's connection to them by giving him a policeman's cap. George wears the hat with pride. He has had experiences based on people seeing him wearing this symbol of authority, the police hat.

One day he was driving on the freeway and a driver, obviously in a hurry, came speeding up from behind him. This speeding man was weaving from lane to lane, wherever he saw an opening that would get him ahead of other cars. When this speedster pulled alongside George, preparing to dart into the spot in front of him, he saw the hat. George saw a look of fear come on the man's face. He did pull in front of George's car, but after he did, he slowed down to the legal speed limit and stayed in front of George's car for the rest of his time on the freeway.

That recognition of authority happened to George several times. But the thing is: George has the look of authority, with the police hat, but he has neither authority nor power. He has not been delegated to enforce the law. He does not have any tools of power: no baton, gun, training, or skills. If he gets in trouble, he does not have the police department to back him up. And he doesn't have an assignment.

Are we like George? When people look at us, do we have the look of authority? We wear crosses and t-shirts proclaiming the gospel. I've seen some great t-shirts, like the one which says, "It takes guts to make a change." Another one is the quote falsely attributed

197

to St. Francis Assissi, "Preach the gospel at all times, use words when necessary." In that way, we are like George. We have the look of authority. But let's be more than George. We have been delegated and have power to call on. We have divine backup and an awesome assignment. We are people of authority.

You have authority. Jesus gave us authority and a charge to share the gospel. Matthew 28:18–20 says you are authorized to go and make disciples. Baptize and teach them. See also Mark 16:15–18 and Luke 10:19 about your authority. These verses, which shout out to us, did not come cheap. Because Jesus shed His blood on the cross, we can receive Jesus as savior, with full benefits. The reason Jesus came was to seek and save the lost (Luke 19:10, NIV). Jesus died in our place, made us right in God's eyes, and brought us into the right relationship with God (Romans 5:8–11, NIV). Jesus destroyed death and in Him we have life and immortality (2 Timothy 1:10, NIV).

We have a commission to go everywhere, loving people in the name of Jesus and training them up in the way they should go. Take heart! Heaven awaits us! All those who believe that Jesus is the Son of God can have victory over sin and the devil (John 16:33, NIV). How? Call on God. "If you confess with your mouth, 'Jesus is Lord,' and believe in your heart that God raised him from the dead, you will be saved" (Romans 10:9, NIV).

God the Father loves His Son and has given everything to Him, including the responsibility of the cross (John 3:35–36, NIV). Likewise, on that Sunday night of Jesus' resurrection, He came to His disciples and said, "Peace be with you! As the Father has sent me, I am sending you" (John 20:21). And then He said, "Receive the Holy Spirit" (John 20:22, NIV). That is where we get our backup. We got the Holy Spirit. Jesus had the Holy Spirit, and He accomplished miracles (John 1:32–34, NIV).

With the Holy Spirit's power, Jesus healed diseases. The woman with the issue of blood was healed, and so was the man who was carried on a mat by four of the man's friends (Mark 5:25–30; Luke 5:17–25, NIV). When Jesus cast a demon out of a man, all the people were amazed and said to each other, "What is this teaching? With authority and power he gives orders to evil spirits and they come out" (Luke 4:31–36, NIV)! In his letter to the Romans, Paul talks about the power of the Spirit. Paul performed signs and miracles and led the Gentiles to obey God (Romans 15:18–19, NIV). We have the same Holy Spirit inside us as Jesus and Paul had working through them. There is only one Holy Spirit (1 Corinthians 12:4–11, NIV).

What about Holy Spirit?

God's way to mature Christians is by praising Him, thanking Him, and speaking in tongues. Holy Spirit helps us with each of these. I experience joy and empowerment in my relationship with Holy Spirit. I advise and urge you to get closer to Holy Spirit by speaking in tongues. Or speak in tongues more than you do now.

If you're asking, "*What is speaking in tongues?*" The short answer is you speak in a language you don't understand. The only ones who understand are Holy Spirit and those to whom Holy Spirit gives understanding.

To be able to speak in tongues, you need to:

1. Want it

2. Ask God for it (Luke 11:11–13, NIV).

3. Drop your desire for control.

4. Relax. Take a deep breath. Open your mouth. Exhale whatever sounds come out. Don't force it. Let it. Don't manufacture it. Look inside yourself at Holy Spirit and trust Him.

What are we doing when we speak in tongues?

1 Corinthians 14 (NIV) is a discussion on the gifts of prophecy and speaking in tongues. There are six things it says we are doing

when we speak in tongues. We are speaking to God. We are uttering mysteries with our spirit. We are building ourselves up spiritually. Our spirit is praying. We are praising God with our spirit. We are giving thanks well.

Do you want to do more of even one of those things? Do you want to speak to God more? Do you want to be linked with the mysteries of God? Do you want to build yourself up spiritually? On top of all that, you are praying, praising God, and giving thanks. Do you want to grow up? Speaking in tongues is like having a double banana split with extra toppings without the calories or insulin drop: A divine wonder. That's the best way I can describe it. As a follower of Jesus Christ, He has already authorized you. We have an assignment to introduce and disciple people to Jesus.

Do you know God's power? By His power, God works in and through us. May God watch over you, guiding your steps so you can accomplish great deeds for His glory.

Endnotes

1.Art Blajos, *Blood In, Blood Out*, (Oxford: Monarch Books, 1996), 125.

2.Nathan Cherry, "Neurobiologist Tells Senate Committee Unborn Babies Feel Pain," *Illinois Family Institute*, July 11, 2013, https://illinoisfamily.org/life/neurobiologist-tells-senate-committee-unborn-babies-feel-pain-at-20-weeks/.

3.Willie J. Parker, "Why I Provide Abortions," Opinion, *New York Times*, November 18, 2016.

4."Our Mission," *Love In the Name of Christ* online, July 21, 2021, https://www.loveinthenameofchrist.org/our-mission/.

5.Warren Marcus, *The Priestly Prayer of the Blessing: The Ancient Secret of the Only Prayer in the Bible Written by God Himself* (Lake Mary: Charisma Media, 2018), xvi.

6.Ibid, 214–217.

7.Mike Murdock, *101 Wisdom Keys* (Cary, NC: Wisdom International, 1994).

8.Teresa Neumann, "Amazing Dreams and Visions Coming Out of the Middle East," *Breaking Christian News*, November 29, 2010, https://www.breakingchristiannews.com/articles/ display_art.html?ID=8430.

9.Jason Gray, "More Like Falling in Love," track 1 on *Everything Sad is Coming Untrue*, Centricity, 2009, compact disc.

10.Tina Turner, "What's Love Got to Do with It," track 2 on *Private Dancer*, Capitol, 1984, compact disc.

11.Newsboys, "We Believe," track 11 on *Restart*, Sparrow, 2013, compact disc.

12.MercyMe, "Even If," track 5 on *Lifer*, Fair Trade, 2017, compact disc.

13.Ron Carpenter Jr, *The Necessity of an Enemy: How the Battle You Face Is Your Best Opportunity* (Colorado Springs: Waterbrook, 2012).

14.Sonny and Julie Arguinzoni, *Treasures Out of Darkness,* (Bloomington: Xlibris, 2011) eBook.

15.Scott Montgomery, "The Exact Amount Needed," *The Burning Bush* (blog), Ed Wrather, March 14, 2002, https://www.theburningbush.org/30.html.

16.Katie Leslie, "French consul in Atlanta: 'No fear' of terrorists," *Atlanta Journal-Constitution*, November 16, 2015, https://www.ajc.com/news/local-govt--politics/french-consul-atlanta-fear-terrorists/ZCM7v4q6mmivq8qw0SoUpI/.

17.Jesus Culture, "'The Holy Spirit Is In You' Bill Johnson," YouTube video, December 4, 2015. https://youtu.be/nYR8ZTvihiU.

18.Duncan Campbell, "Mountaineer trapped by boulder amputated arm with a pocketknife," The Guardian, May 2, 2003, https://www.theguardian.com/world/2003/may/03/duncancampbell.

19.Petra, "Jesus, Friend of Sinners," track 6 on Revival, EMI Studios, 2001, compact disc.

20.Mark Andrew Olsen, *The Watchers*, (Ada, MI: Baker, 2008).

21.Ibid.

22.Ibid.

23.Oswald Chambers, *So I Send You/Workmen of God: Recognizing and Answering God's Call to Service*, (MI: Discovery House Publishing, 1993).

24.Heather Preston Wheeler, "A Miracle of the Heart," *Northwest Adventists Gleaner*, October 1, 2009, https://nwadventists.com/feature/miracle-heart.

25.Billy Graham, *Angels: God's Secret Agents*, (NY: Doubleday & Company, 1975).

26.Aimee Herd, "Miracle of an Obedient Heart at the I-35 Bridge," *Breaking Christian News*, August 10, 2007, https://www.breakingchristiannews.com/articles/display_art.html?ID=43 02.

27.Ibid.

Bibliography

Arguinzoni, Sonny & Julie. *Treasures Out of Darkness*. Green Forest, AR: New Leaf, 1991.

Blajos, Art and Keith Wilkerson. *Blood In, Blood Out*. n.p.: Monarch Books, 1996.

Campbell, Duncan. "Mountaineer trapped by boulder amputated arm with a pocketknife," *The Guardian*, May 2, 2003. https://www.theguardian.com/world/2003/may/03/duncancampb ell.

Chambers, Oswald. *So Send I You / Workmen of God: Recognizing and Answering God's Call to Service*. Grand Rapids: Discovery House Publishing, 1993.

Cherry, Nathan. "Neurobiologist Tells Senate Committee Unborn Babies Feel Pain at 20 Weeks," *Illinois Family Institute*, June 11, 2013. https://illinoisfamily.org/life/neurobiologist.

Graham, Billy. *Angels: God's Secret Agents*. New York City: Doubleday & Company, 1975.

Gray, Jason. "More Like Falling in Love," track 1 on *Everything Sad is Coming Untrue*, Centricity, 2009, compact disc.

Herd, Aimee. "The Miracle of an Obedient Heart at the I-35 Bridge," *Breaking Christian News*, August 10, 2007. https://www.breakingchristiannews.com/articles/display_art.html?ID=4302.

Hybels, Bill. *Just Walk Across the Room: Simple Steps Pointing People to Faith*. Grand Rapids: Zondervan, 2006.

Johnson, Bill. *When Heaven Invades Earth: A Practical Guide to a Life of Miracles*. Shippensburg, PA: Destiny Image, 2005.

Leslie, Katie. "French consul in Atlanta: 'No fear' of terrorists," *Atlanta Journal-Constitution*, November 16, 2015. https://www.ajc.com/news/local-govt--politics/french-consul-atlanta-fear-terrorists/ZCM7v4q6mmivq8qw0SoUpI/.

Marcus, Warren M. *The Priestly Prayer of the Blessing: The Ancient Secret of the Only Prayer in the Bible Written by God Himself*. Lake Mary, FL: Charisma House, 2018.

MercyMe. "Even If," track 5 on *Lifer*, Fair Trade, 2017, compact disc.

Montgomery, Scott. 2002. "The Exact Amount Needed." *The Burning Bush* (blog). Ed Wrather. March 14. https://www.theburningbush.org/30.html.

Murdock, Mike. *101 Wisdom Keys*. Cary, NC: Wisdom International, 1994.

Neumann, Teresa. "Amazing Dreams and Visions Coming Out of the Middle East," *Breaking Christian News*, November 29, 2010. https://www.breakingchristiannews.com/articles/di splay_art.html?ID=8430.

Newsboys. "We Believe," track 11 on *Restar*, Sparrow Records, 2013, compact disc.

Wheeler, Heather P. "A Miracle of the Heart," *Gleaner*, October 1, 2009. https://nwadventi sts.com/feature/miracle-heart.

"Our Mission." Love In the Name of Christ, accessed July 21, 2021, https://www.loveinthename ofchrist.org/our-mission/.

Olsen, Mark A. *The Watchers*. Ada, MI: Baker, 2008.

Parker, Willie J. 2015. "Why I Provide Abortions." *New York Times*. November 18. https://www. nytimes.com/2015/11/18/opinion/why-i-provide-abortions.html.

Petra, "Jesus, Friend of Sinners," track 6 on *Revival*, EMI Studios, 2001, compact disc.

Piper, Don. *90 Minutes in Heaven: A True Story of Death and Life*. Grand Rapids: Revell. 2004.

Turner, Tina. "What's Love Got to Do with It," track 3 on *Private Dancer*, Capitol Records, 1984, compact disc.

Warren, Rick. *The Purpose Driven Life: What on Earth Am I Here For?* Grand Rapids: Zondervan, 2002.

CPSIA information can be obtained
at www.ICGtesting.com
Printed in the USA
LVHW080256220122
709011LV00011B/322

9 781637 699607